V. Theune. Nyachote
fer da Medal deVatrick
a.h bu.
25. 11. '06

LECTIO DIVINA WITH THE SUNDAY GOSPELS

Michel de Verteuil

Lectio Divina with the Sunday Gospels

THE YEAR OF LUKE – YEAR C

the columba press

First published in 2004 by
ᴄhe ᴄoʟuмʙᴀ pʀᴇss
55A Spruce Avenue, Stillorgan Industrial Park,
Blackrock, Co Dublin

Cover by Bill Bolger
Origination by The Columba Press
Printed in Ireland by ColourBooks Ltd, Dublin

ISBN 1 85607 440 4

Contents

Introduction

Lectio Divina: A method of biblical reflection
The reflections proposed in this book are the fruit of lectio divina, a method of meditative Bible reading which goes back to the early centuries of our church, and continues to be a source of deep spiritual growth for many people throughout the world.

Lectio divina (a Latin expression which means sacred reading) is done in three stages:

- Reading: you read the passage slowly and reverentially, allowing the words to sink into your consciousness;
- Meditation: you allow the passage to stir up memories within you, so that you recognise in it your own experience or that of people who have touched your life;
- Prayer: you allow the meditation to lead you to prayer – thanksgiving, humility and petition.

The prayers given here, week by week, are intended to serve as models. You can use them as they are, but they will also suggest ways in which you can pray from your own meditations.

Now and then, prayers will be preceded by quotations from well known thinkers or spiritual writers. The quotations are there to remind us that through Bible reading we enter into the wisdom of the entire human family.

The basic principle of lectio divina is that Bible reading is a personal encounter with God, a communion which resembles (though different from) the communion of the Eucharist. This goes against what has prevailed in our church for some centuries: the text was seen as containing a message – doctrinal or moral – and once we got the message, the text had achieved its purpose. In lectio divina, we love the text, linger over it, read it over and over, let it remain with us.

When we approach the text in this way, we come face to face with the fact that it speaks to the imagination. A Bible text is not like a textbook or a newspaper, providing us with objective information. It was not written like that. Instead, it stirs up feelings; we find ourselves identifying with the characters – we feel for them, admire them or dislike them. We are caught up in the movement of the text, its suspense, its dramatic reversals of fortune, its unanswered questions.

Gradually, we 'recognise' the text; we find that we have lived the sequence of events ourselves, or have seen them lived in others who have touched our lives, for good or for ill. Reading the text becomes a homecoming – and a lifting up. We find ourselves caught up in the story of God's people, 'fellow citizens with the saints' (Eph 2:19); we are the lowly ones whom God 'lifts up from the dust and sets in the company of princes, yes the princes of his people' (Ps 113:7-8).

Lectio divina, like all imaginative communication – especially storytelling – teaches not directly but by changing the consciousness of those who practise it. By identifying ourselves with God's people – Jesus, the prophets and the great men and women of the Old and New Testaments – we find ourselves adopting their attitudes. We also recognise ourselves in the bad characters of the text – the Pharisees, Pharaoh, the apostles when they were jealous of each other – and find that we want to give up these attitudes.

The Bible, recognised as coinciding with our experience, reveals to us the truth about life – not abstract truth, but an ideal we hunger and thirst for and, from another perspective, an evil we recoil from. In the Bible text, therefore, we discover the double reality of every human person – a story of sin and a story of grace. They are not equally true, however – the story of grace is the deep truth of the person, their 'true name', the wheat which God will gather into his barn; sin is the chaff that will be burnt in a fire that never goes out (cf Mt 3:12).

Lectio blossoms spontaneously into prayer in three dimensions:

• Thanksgiving that Jesus is alive in the story of grace;
• Humility that the story of sin is alive;
• Petition that the story of grace may prevail – 'Come, Lord Jesus!'

In lectio divina we experience the true meaning of theology – entering through Bible reading into the wisdom of God or, more accurately, allowing God-alive-in-the-Bible to lead us into wisdom, humbly, gratefully and with awe, like St Paul on the road to Damascus. The wisdom of God gives us his perspective on every aspect of life: one-to-one relationships, but also economics, politics, agriculture, etc.

Lectio divina is best taught and practised with the church's Sunday lectionary as it was reformed after the Second Vatican Council. It has its shortcomings, but overall it is a wonderfully constructed three-year programme in Bible reading. By being faithful to the lectionary in this way, we experience ourselves in communion with the church and, through the church, with all humanity, sharing in the grace and the sin of our contemporaries. We can say of Bible reading what St Paul says of the Eucharist: 'We, though many, form one body because we partake of the one bread' (1 Cor 10:17).

These gospel meditations for the Sundays of St Luke's Year will be followed in due course by similar reflections on the readings for the Sundays of Years A and B.

I would like to thank all who have helped me with them, especially Elena Lombardi-French in Dublin and Brendan Clifford OP in Limerick. Without their help and active encouragement these reflections would never have been published.

Advent: The Mystery of Waiting

Advent is the liturgical season when we pay special attention to the mystery of waiting. We have a real problem here because most of us don't like waiting, we don't see it as something to celebrate. In fact this may well be one of the reasons why people don't understand Advent correctly – although it may also be true that not celebrating it as we should has led us to misunderstand the value of waiting.

Whereas waiting bores and often irritates us, the Bible teaches us that if we approach it in the right spirit, waiting is a creative moment when we grow spiritually. When we wait we are in touch with an essential aspect of our humanity which is that we are dependent on God and on one another. It is also an act of love since, by waiting for others, we pay them the respect of letting them be free.

Waiting is a mystery – God waits and nature waits – so that when we as individuals wait we go beyond ourselves and enter into a sacred life-giving process, experiencing that we are made in the image and likeness of God. This is why Advent is a time of celebration. It is the season when we remember with gratitude creative experiences of waiting in our lives or the lives of people we have known, the people who have waited for us at one time or another. We also remember the great waiting experiences in human history, in the Bible, and especially in the life of Jesus.

But we must also make Advent a time of teaching. During this season all those involved in the work of Christian education, whether as catechists or preachers or guides, should explore the mystery of waiting: true and false ways of waiting, the danger of not knowing how to wait, ascetical practices that will help us wait more creatively.

Finally, waiting can be, as we know from our own experience, a time of suffering and sometimes of despair. In Advent, we make a special effort to feel for those who are crying out in their agony, 'How long, O Lord?' – those we can name and the countless others 'whose faith is known to God alone'. Through our meditation we can let the special grace of the season flow through us to these brothers and sisters of ours, turning their mourning into dancing and their time of barrenness into one of abundance and fertility.

The liturgy of the word is a teaching moment. It is not abstract teaching, where truths are presented to be learnt, but teaching by celebration. We celebrate biblical stories which exemplify the spirit of the particular season, identifying with the persons in them. In the process we learn more about biblical values, experience repentance as we become more aware of how we (and the whole church) have failed to practise those values, and pray that we will enter more fully into God's plan for us – that his kingdom will come. The main person we identify with is Jesus himself. At each liturgical season we celebrate one particular stage of his life on earth, not as a past event but as a way in which he continues to live among us.

The grace of Advent is hope, the virtue by which we human beings can recognise and welcome God present in the world but not experienced with our senses. The corresponding stage in Jesus' life which we celebrate in this season is when he was in the womb of Mary. It was a time in the history of salvation when the Word was made flesh, but was not visible, his presence was real but an object of hope, like the tiny mustard seed which we trust will eventually become a great tree in whose branches the birds of the air will shelter.

The fruit of Advent then is that we grow in the virtue of hope that God is present even when he is hidden. We are undaunted by evil, do not give up on our dreams, face with confidence the present historical moment (ours, that of our society and of the modern world), welcome the people he sends us, and help them get in touch with the best in themselves – where God is present.

In celebrating Jesus in the womb of Mary we celebrate all the times, in the Bible and in history, when human beings have been invited by God to recognise his hidden presence in the world. The liturgical readings for the season then present us with biblical persons who are models of hope.

The Bible teaches this through stories, not abstract definitions. It does not attempt to define what hope is, but invites us to meditate on people of hope. We celebrate them and enter into their attitudes, how they interpreted the events of their time and how they related to their contemporaries.

By doing this we celebrate our own experiences of hope, in ourselves and others. In the process we experience conversion, renew our hope which had grown cold. We also pray that those in despair will turn to hope and we commit ourselves to bringing hope into the world.

First Sunday of Advent

Gospel Reading: Luke 21:25-28, 34-36

25Jesus said to his disciples: 'There will be signs in the sun and moon and stars; on earth nations in agony, bewildered by the clamour of the ocean and its waves; 26men dying of fear as they await what menaces the world, for the powers of heaven will be shaken. 27And then they will see the Son of Man coming in a cloud with power and great glory. 28When these things begin to take place, stand erect, hold your heads high, because your liberation is near at hand. 34Watch yourselves, or your hearts will be coarsened with debauchery and drunkenness and the cares of life, and that day will be sprung on you suddenly, like a trap. 35For it will come down on every living man on the face of the earth. 36Stay awake, praying at all times for the strength to survive all that is going to happen, and to stand with confidence before the Son of Man.'

The gospel readings for Advent each year invite us to meditate on the mystery of waiting, and they do it by presenting us with stories of great people who knew how to wait.

On the first Sunday, Jesus himself is the model as he taught his followers the spirituality of 'waiting in joyful hope'.

The passage is clearly in two sections, verses 25 to 28, and verses 34 to 36.

You must interpret verses 25 to 28 in the light of your experience, times when your world or the world of your family or other community collapsed. Allow the dramatic language to express this experience, making sure that you recognise the double movement of collapse and rebirth.

If you decide to meditate on verses 34 to 36, the key will be to identify concretely the meaning of 'that day', a time like the one in verses 25 to 28. Then you will get a feel for the teaching of Jesus.

* * *

Lord, great tragedies befall us from time to time:
- we lose our job;
- a spouse proves unfaithful;
- we discover that one of our children is on drugs;
- we fall into a sin we thought we had overcome.

These are moments of great distress. It is as if the sun and moon and stars are no longer there in the heavens. We feel as if we are drowning, the ocean and its clamorous waves overwhelming us. The powers of heaven have been shaken and we are dying of fear as we await the future which menaces us.

But, somehow or other, that moment, terrible as it is, brings its own grace:
- we find we have more courage than we thought;
- our family finds a new unity;
- we forgive a long-standing hurt.

Jesus comes into our lives with power and great glory.
We have learnt now that we need never panic.
When these things begin to take place,
we can stand erect, hold our heads high,
because a moment of grace and liberation is near at hand.

Lord, we thank you for the times when oppressed people can stand erect and hold their heads high because a moment of liberation is near at hand.

'After one time, is two time.' Trinidadian saying.
Lord, at one point in our lives we felt that good times would never end. We lived mindlessly, looking down on others who were less successful or less virtuous.
We thank you for bringing us to our senses:
- we fell sick;
- we fell into a sin we thought we would never commit;
- one of our children got into trouble with the law.

It was Jesus warning us to watch ourselves,
and reminding us that the day of reckoning is always sprung on us like a trap,
for it comes down on every living person on the face of the earth.
Lord, make us aware of how our minds have been coarsened
by over-indulgence and being too much engrossed by the cares of this life.

We know that what counts in life is to be able to stand with confidence before the Son of Man.

Lord, we sometimes think that, as a church community,
we are exempt from the ups and downs of institutions.
But the day of crisis is sprung on us suddenly like a trap,
just as it comes down on every group on the face of the earth.

Second Sunday of Advent

Gospel Reading: Luke 3:1-6

¹In the fifteenth year of Tiberius Caesar's reign, when Pontius Pilate was governor of Judaea, Herod tetrarch of Galilee, his brother Philip tetrarch of the lands of Ituraea and Trachonitis, Lysanias tetrarch of Abilene, ²during the pontificate of Annas and Caiaphas, the word of God came to John son of Zechariah, in the wilderness. ³He went through the whole Jordan district proclaiming a baptism of repentance for the forgiveness of sins, ⁴as it is written in the book of the sayings of the prophet Isaiah:

A voice cries in the wilderness:
Prepare a way for the Lord,
make his paths straight.
⁵Every valley will be filled in,
every mountain and hill be laid low,
winding ways will be straightened
and rough roads made smooth.
⁶And all mankind shall see the salvation of God.

On the second and third Sundays of Advent, the church gives us John the Baptist as a model of someone who knows how to wait. In this first passage we have Luke's summary of the mission of John the Baptist. It is none other than the mission of Jesus himself and of all preachers of the gospel.

In verses 1 and 2 St Luke invites us to meditate on God's word which comes to John in the wilderness, bypassing the powerful ones of the world.

Verse 3 is a concise summary of John's (and Jesus') preaching.

There are two aspects to verses 4 and 5: the fact that John lived out the vocation of Isaiah, and then the content of his preaching expressed in poetic language. We are invited to identify with both aspects.

* * *

'I thank you, Father, for hiding these things from the learned and the
clever and revealing them to mere children.' Luke 10:21

Lord, we forget your way of doing things.
We think it is important to seek the favour of the great ones of
the world,
as if their patronage is necessary for the spread of your gospel,
while we neglect the wisdom of the poor.
But your word has always bypassed
   - Tiberius Caesar reigning for 15 years,
   - Pilate, the great governor,
   - those powerful tetrarchs Herod, Philip and Lysanius,
and come to a humble person, living in the wilderness.

Lord, we remember a time when we were in the wilderness:
   - our family relationships were at their lowest level;
   - at work everything seemed to be going wrong;
   - violence and crime ruled in the country;
   - our prayer life was as dry as dust.
Yet within that very wilderness there was a voice within us,
crying out that things would turn out right.
We felt so sure of this that,
even in the midst of all that desolation,
we prepared a way for your coming
and made the paths straight
so that we would be there to welcome you.
We saw some deep valleys
and wondered how we would ever get across them,
but we knew that every one of them would be filled in.
There were high mountains before us; they would all be laid low.
The road was winding,
so that every time we turned a corner another one appeared;
it would be straightened.
As for the rough roads that had our feet sore and bleeding,
they would become smooth as glass.
We knew for sure that we would experience your salvation.
Thank you, Lord.

'We live in a world where no one cares.' Secondary School principal
Lord, we pray that in our heartless world the church may,
like John the Baptist,
fulfil what is written in the book
of the sayings of the prophet Isaiah,
and be a voice crying out to those who feel themselves
in a wilderness
that you have not abandoned them,
that every valley will be filled in,
every mountain and hill laid low,
winding ways will be straightened
and rough roads made smooth.

'If all people are God's children, why are we rejoicing when our sons and daughters are safe while death and destruction is wreaked upon innocent people?' Religious Superiors of the USA after the Gulf War
Lord, we still need John the Baptist to teach us your will that all
must see your salvation.

'A critical ingredient of the Caribbean today is collective self-knowledge as the vital pre-condition to collective self-possessiveness.' Lloyd Best
Lord, give us the grace to know that what we are doing
is written in the books of the sayings of the prophets.

Third Sunday of Advent

Gospel Reading: Luke 3:10-18

10*When all the people asked John, 'What must we do?'* 11*he answered, 'If anyone has two tunics he must share with the man who has none, and the one who has something to eat must do the same.'* 12*There were tax collectors too who came for baptism, and these said to him, 'Master, what must we do?'* 13*He said to them, 'Exact no more than your rate.'* 14*Some soldiers asked him in their turn, 'What about us? What must we do?' He said to them, 'No intimidation! No extortion! Be content with your pay!'*

15*A feeling of expectancy had grown among the people, who were beginning to think that John might be the Christ,* 16*so John declared before them all, 'I baptise you with water, but someone is coming, someone who is more powerful than I am, and I am not fit to undo the strap of his sandals; he will baptise you with the Holy Spirit and fire.* 17*His winnowing fan is in his hand to clear his threshing floor and to gather the wheat into his barn; but the chaff he will burn in a fire that will never go out.'*

18*As well as this, there were many other things he said to exhort the people and announce the Good News to them.*

On the third Sunday of Advent St Luke gives us a glimpse into the personality of that wonderful person, John the Baptist. In your meditation, let him remind you of great people you have known.

In verses 10 to 14 John speaks openly. Notice how he has a different word for each group which questions him. Notice too how the soldiers feel that even they can get a word of salvation.

Verses 15 to 18 give us a further insight into the kind of person John the Baptist was. He may have said these words in a moment of discouragement, in which case they express his trust that God would complete what was lacking in his ministry. But perhaps they tell us of his humility in the midst of his extraordinary success as a preacher.

* * *

'The bread you do not use is the bread of the hungry.' St Ambrose
Lord, we thank you for people who are direct and honest
like John the Baptist.
When we ask them what we must do,
they don't beat around the bush but tell us openly:
those who have two tunics
must share with those who have none,
and those with something to eat must do the same.
Lord, John the Baptist knew his people.
When the tax collectors came for baptism
he told them exactly what they must do,
and so too with the soldiers.
Lord, we pray for the church today.

'We all want to be famous people, but the moment we want to be something we are no longer free.' Krishnamurti
Lord, give us the humility of John the Basptist.
When a feeling of expectancy grows
and our followers begin to think
that we might be some kind of Messiah,
help us to declare before them all
that we are merely baptising with water.
There is one who is more powerful than we are
and he baptises with the Holy Spirit and with fire.

'We are a resourceful people but deadly scared of our own natively-inspired success.' Clifford Sealey, Trinidadian poet
Lord, often we do not accomplish what we can
because we are afraid of failure.
We must be content to baptise with water,
trusting that someone will come after us
who is more powerful than we are,
and he will baptise with the Holy Spirit and with fire.

'Something happened between me and the earth. The land recognised me.' Earl Lovelace as he landed on African soil for the first time, November 1991

Lord, we thank you for the moments of grace
when we feel we are connected
with the whole of creation and all of our history.
We know then that your winnowing fan is in your hand,
that evil is merely chaff
which you will burn in a fire that will never go out,
whereas we are your precious wheat
which you will gather into your barn.

Fourth Sunday of Advent

Gospel Reading: Luke 1:39-44

39Mary set out and went as quickly as she could to a town in the hill country of Judah. 40She went into Zechariah's house and greeted Elizabeth. 41Now as soon as Elizabeth heard Mary's greeting, the child leapt in her womb and Elizabeth was filled with the Holy Spirit. 42She gave a loud cry and said, 'Of all women you are the most blessed, and blessed is the fruit of your womb. Why should I be honoured with a visit from the mother of my Lord? 43For the moment your greeting reached my ears, the child in my womb leapt for joy. 44Yes, blessed is she who believed that the promise made her by the Lord would be fulfilled.'

Each year the gospel passage for this Sunday is a story of Mary's pregnancy, and for this year it is the visitation. We meditate on this story as the second joyful mystery of the rosary, so that this could be an opportunity to go into it deeper than we usually can in saying the rosary; this would give depth to the way we say that prayer, which plays an important part in the lives of many people.

It is the story of two pregnant women and, therefore, an opportunity to enter into the symbolism of that experience, especially for those who have gone through it, seeing it as a symbol of how waiting can be a creative time, one when we express our love and one also when we can unmask all the self-centredness that is latent within us and blocks our ability to give ourselves wholeheartedly to others. Of course, it could also be a meditation on the sacredness of pregnancy itself.

Mary should be the main focus of our attention, symbol at this moment of her life of the person of faith, and indeed of the church. Particularly significant is the expression 'blessed' that is attributed to her by Elizabeth; we must give the word its full biblical meaning, indicating that a person has a great gift from God and also that he or she has brought blessings to others. Mary's blessedness in this passage is simply that she has faith, no great achievements or visible signs of God's favour – just faith.

* * *

Lord, there was a time when we had a dream:
  - one day we would finally succeed in giving up drugs or
  drink and lead a healthy, creative life;
  - we would develop a talent for music we knew we had but
  had never been recognised;
  - we would be friends with someone we were too shy even to
  speak to;
  - we would play our part in making our country a more
  human and caring place.
The dream was there within us but very small,
so that people looking at us would think
that we would never change.
Then someone like Mary came into our lives,
someone who also had a dream within her
and so understood us.
There was something in her greeting
– not what she said,
just the tone of her greeting as it reached our ears –
and in an instant the dream within us came alive,
like John the Baptist leaping for joy in the womb of Elizabeth.
We felt confident that it would become a reality one day
and we and the world would be different.
It was like being visited by a mother,
not just an ordinary mother,
but one who was giving birth to the presence of God.
A deep feeling of humility came over us;
we felt blessed and filled with the Holy Spirit.

Lord, we think today of some girl who is pregnant
and regrets this pregnancy.
Perhaps she has no one in the home to lean on;
perhaps she is over-burdened with financial problems
or finds that the child will block her career.
We ask you to send some Mary to visit her home,
someone who has problems too
but trusts that you will fulfil the hopes she has within her,
and who will greet her in such a way
that the child in her womb will leap for joy
and she will feel blessed and filled with your Holy Spirit.

Lord, as a church, we have achievements that we are proud of,
great resources too that others admire us for:
    - schools that many parents want to send their children to;
    - an international network from which we get encourage-
    ment and financial support;
    - an ancient and highly respected spiritual tradition and a
    host of great saints to whom we turn as personal friends.
But all that can make us arrogant.
Help us rather to be like Mary,
remembering that others have resources too,
other churches, other faiths, other groups in society,
so that we may visit them
as Mary visited Elizabeth in the hill country,
not with an ulterior motive or condescendingly,
but just to greet them
so that the moment the sound of our greeting reaches their ears
they will rejoice in their gifts and in ours too.

Lord,
there is a blessedness by which we experience great favours
– when we pass an examination,
get a promotion or overcome some bad habit.
Help us to recognise the blessedness of Mary
that makes us the most blessed of all
when we trust that the promises you make us will be fulfilled.
Great and wonderful things are born
from that kind of blessedness.

Lord, we thank you for mothers in our country
who had to struggle so hard to bring up their children well,
and in spite of great odds
have managed their homes with dignity.
What kept them going was a faith like Mary's,
the deep belief that you had planted
certain convictions within them
and that these would be vindicated.
We have been blessed by having them among us,
and many great people have been born
as the fruit of their wombs.

The Nativity of Our Lord

Gospel reading: Luke 2:1-20

[1]Now at this time Caesar Augustus issued a decree for a census of the whole world to be taken. [2]This census – the first – took place while Quirinius was governor of Syria, [3]and everyone went to his own town to be registered. [4]So Joseph set out from the town of Nazareth in Galilee and travelled up to Judaea, to the town of David called Bethlehem, since he was of David's House and line, [5]in order to be registered together with Mary, his betrothed, who was with child. [6]While they were there the time came for her to have her child, [7]and she gave birth to a son, her first-born. She wrapped him in swaddling clothes and laid him in a manger because there was no room for them at the inn.

[8]In the countryside close by there were shepherds who lived in the fields and took it in turns to watch their flocks during the night. [9]The angel of the Lord appeared to them and the glory of the Lord shone round them. They were terrified, [10]but the angel said, 'Do not be afraid. Listen, I bring you news of great joy, a joy to be shared by the whole people. [11]Today in the town of David a saviour has been born to you; he is Christ the Lord. [12]And here is a sign for you: you will find a baby wrapped in swaddling clothes and lying in a manger.' [13]And suddenly with the angel there was a great throng of the heavenly host, praising God and singing: [14]'Glory to God in the highest heaven, and peace to men who enjoy his favour.' [15]Now when the angels had gone from them into heaven, the shepherds said to one another, 'Let us go to Bethlehem and see this thing that has happened which the Lord has made known to us.' [16]So they hurried away and found Mary and Joseph, and the baby lying in the manger. [17]When they saw the child they repeated what they had been told about him, [18]and everyone who heard it was astonished at what the shepherds had to say.

[19]As for Mary, she treasured all these things and pondered them in her heart. [20]And the shepherds went back glorifying and praising God for all they had heard and seen; it was exactly as they had been told.

This well-known story is very rich so we will focus on some aspects only, staying with Mary's perspective, especially in verses 6 to 7, and 16 to 20.

In verses 6 and 7 Luke tells us that Mary gave birth 'when the

time came for her to have her child.' Contrary to the popular interpretation, he indicates no regret that there was no room in the
inn. All happened as was foretold.

To understand the significance of verse 19, it is important to
note that the Greek word which we translate as 'things' is *rhema*,
which means both 'word' and 'event'. Mary, through her interior
attitude of respectful listening, turns the event into a sacred
word.

* * *

'Nothing happens before its time.' Trinidadian saying
Lord, we pray for those who are involved in lofty projects and
are becoming impatient:
    - parish youth leaders who are not getting co-operation;
    - a new party that has won no seats in the elections;
    - parents who are trying in vain to dialogue with their
    teenagers.
Help them to remember Mary and how, when the time came for
her to have her child, she gave birth to a son.
She was at peace, felt no great concern
that there was no room for them in the inn,
merely wrapped her child in swaddling cloths
and laid him in a manger.

Lord, these days we are all very busy.
At work or in school
we have to expend much effort to achieve success.
At home we are bombarded with information
from television and radio.
We have time only for the sensational
and we allow the ordinary events of life to come and go:
    - the signs of maturity in our children;
    - the life crises of those close to us;
    - new stirrings of resentment or of hope among ordinary peo-
    ple in our country.
Even in our relationship with you
we concentrate on the miraculous
and the extraordinary, glorify and praise you
because things turn out exactly as we were told they would.

Mary teaches us, on the contrary,
to see in every event a call to grow,
a sacred word you speak to us,
to be welcomed as a treasure and pondered in our hearts,
reflected on and integrated into our consciousness.
Lord, help us to be more like Mary.

'My cell will not be one of stone or wood, but of self-knowledge.'
St Catherine of Siena
Lord, we thank you for all the contemplatives in the world,
those in enclosed convents, and those called, like Mary,
to live in their families and in secular surroundings.
While others chatter
and repeat endlessly what they have been told,
these, like Mary, know how to be silent,
treasuring things and pondering them in their hearts.

The Holy Family

41*Every year his parents used to go to Jerusalem for the feast of the Passover.* 42*When he was twelve years old, they went up for the feast as usual.* 43*When they were on their way home after the feast, the boy Jesus stayed behind in Jerusalem without his parents knowing it.* 44*They assumed he was with the caravan, and it was only after a day's journey that they went to look for him among their relations and acquaintances.* 45*When they failed to find him they went back to Jerusalem looking for him everywhere.*

46*Three days later, they found him in the Temple, sitting among the doctors, listening to them, and asking them questions;* 47*and all those who heard him were astounded at his intelligence and his replies.*

48*They were overcome when they saw him, and his mother said to him, 'My child, why have you done this to us? See how worried your father and I have been, looking for you.'* 49*'Why were you looking for me?' he replied. 'Did you not know that I must be busy with my Father's affairs?'* 50*But they did not understand what he meant.*

51*He then went down with them and came to Nazareth and lived under their authority. His mother stored up all these things in her heart.* 52*And Jesus increased in wisdom, in stature, and in favour with God and men.*

Here is a highly symbolic story. We can read it from Jesus' point of view or from that of his parents.

We can divide the story into two parts – verses 41 to 50, and verses 51 and 52 – and meditate on each separately. Taken together, however, and understood as complementing each other, they give us a balanced picture of the role of authority in human life.

* * *

Lord, we pray today for all those involved in the work of education – parents, teachers, youth leaders, church ministers.
Young people come to stay with us
and live under our authority for a time,
increasing in wisdom, in stature
and in favour with you and with men and women.
But they are not ours.
You are their father and they must be busy about your affairs.
Some have unusual vocations –
in the church perhaps, or in the arts, or in politics.
At times we will feel we have lost them
and we will be overcome with worry
as we spend days looking for them.
Then, quite unexpectedly, we find them, at ease in their temple,
asking and answering questions,
quite surprised that we should be looking for them,
while we remain perplexed at what it all means.
Lord, bringing up children is a lofty calling.
Help us, like Mary and Joseph, to be faithful to it.

'It may be that the salvation of the world lies with the maladjusted.'
Martin Luther King
Lord, there are times in life when we must step out on our own,
knowing that dear ones will be very worried, looking for us,
wanting to bring us back to Nazareth
where we can be subject to them.
Give us the grace to commit ourselves, like Jesus,
to what we know to be our Father's business.

*'The church must be concerned not just with herself and her relation-
ship of union with God, but with human beings as they really are
today.'* Pope Paul VI concluding the Second Vatican Council, December 1965
Lord, as a church we tend to remain within our concerns,
safe in Nazareth where we know the rules of the game,
who is subject to whom,
and we can feel sure we are growing in wisdom, in stature,
and in favour with God
and with the influential people in society.

We pray that your church may take the risk
of being lost for days at a time,
even though its leaders are overcome with worry,
so that Jesus can be among the learned people of our time,
listening to them and asking them questions,
and modern generations, like previous ones, can be astounded
by the wisdom of his message
and of the replies he brings to the problems of our time.

> *'Only one ship is seeking us, a black-*
> *sailed unfamiliar, towing at her back*
> *a huge and birdless silence. In her wake*
> *no waters breed or break.'* West Indian poem

Lord, when we are young we have lofty goals for ourselves.
We are in Jerusalem, at the centre of things,
questioning the wisdom of our day
and astounding all by the intelligence of our replies.
Then another time comes when we find ourselves stagnant,
not going anywhere or achieving anything,
subject to the conventions and prejudices of society.
Teach us, Lord, that this too is a necessary stage
when, like Jesus in Nazareth, we can increase in wisdom,
in stature and in favour with you.

Second Sunday after Christmas

Gospel reading: John 1:1-18

[1]In the beginning was the Word: the Word was with God and the Word was God. [2]He was with God in the beginning. [3]Through him all things came to be, not one thing had its being but through him. [4]All that came to be had life in him and that life was the light of men, [5]a light that shines in the dark, a light that darkness could not overpower.

[6]A man came, sent by God. His name was John. [7]He came as a witness, as a witness to speak for the light, so that everyone might believe through him. [8]He was not the light, only a witness to speak for the light. [9]The Word was the true light that enlightens all men; and he was coming into the world. [10]He was in the world that had its being through him, and the world did not know him. [11]He came to his own domain and his own people did not accept him. [12]But to all who did accept him he gave power to become children of God, to all who believe in the name of him [13]who was born not out of human stock or urge of the flesh or will of man but of God himself. [14]The Word was made flesh, he lived among us, and we saw his glory, the glory that is his as the only Son of the Father, full of grace and truth.

[15]John appears as his witness. He proclaims: 'This is the one of whom I said: He who comes after me ranks before me because he existed before me.' [16]Indeed, from his fulness we have, all of us, received – yes, grace in return for grace, [17]since, though the Law was given through Moses, grace and truth have come through Jesus Christ. [18]No one has ever seen God; it is the only Son, who is nearest to the Father's heart, who has made him known.

This passage is the prologue to St John's gospel, a very deep teaching on the mystery of the incarnation. But do not let yourself be intimidated by the depth; remember that it was written for you; like the whole Bible, it was 'for you and for your salvation that it came down from heaven.'

It may be helpful to divide the passage as follows:

Verse 1: The Word of God which was made flesh had his beginnings with God before creation. Identify what in your experience was an incarnation of the Word and then remember when you knew that this word was with God from all eternity.

Verses 2-5: The story of creation, understood as an ongoing process.

Verses 6-8: the vocation of John the Baptist; recognise in him the vocation of all great people.

Verses 9-14: St John's presentation of the incarnation. Recognise the mystery from your own experience, in particular the strange mystery of the one who made and sustains humanity being rejected by this same humanity.

Verses 16-18: A further meditation on the mystery of the incarnation. Note especially the process of growth 'from grace to grace', and the difference between Jesus and all others.

* * *

'To the end of our lives the Bible remains an unexplored and unsubdued land full of concealed wonders and choice treasures.' Cardinal Newman

Lord, we thank you for the deep moments of Bible reading
when we knew that we were in the presence of a Word
which existed from the beginning before time began,
which was with you before you created the world,
which was truly divine, with you from the beginning,
and which was made flesh and was living among us.

'In meditation I pass through my body which exists in time and space, and beyond my thoughts which reflect my body-consciousness. I discover my ground in the Word, my real self which exists eternally in God and with God.' Bede Griffiths

Lord, we thank you for the moments of deep prayer
when we knew that we have life in your Word,
that Word which was in the beginning,
which was with you and was you.

Lord, humanity today wants to live independently of you,
and even Christians speak as if you created the world
and then left it to its own devices.
We thank you for the teaching of St John
reminding us that all things come to be
only because you speak a Word,
and that every single thing that exists today

has its being because that Word continues to be spoken in it,
and the only way that anything
which has come to be has life today
is because your Word lives within it.

'Perestroika shows that there are some live cells still left in our society,
battling against the disintegration of the Spirit.' A Russian writer
Lord, we thank you that the human spirit is unconquerable,
it is a light that comes from you,
a light that continues to shine even when there is great darkness,
a light that no darkness can overcome.

'Far from being the ultimate measure of all things, human beings can
only realise themselves by reaching beyond themselves.'
Paul VI, *Populorum progressio*
Lord, how true it is
that we can only find our dignity as your sons and daughters
if we believe that there is more to us than a human birth,
the urges of the flesh and the human will
and that within us your love is at work.

'Of all the crimes of colonialism there is none worse that the attempt to
make us believe that we had no indigenous culture of our own.' Julius
Nyerere
Lord, we pray that as Christians
we may live the message of the incarnation,
that your eternal Word was made flesh,
so that in every culture you are at work,
and if we look at our past in the light of faith
we will see your glory, Jesus at work in our history,
full of grace and truth.

Lord, a conversion experience is always a home-coming:
  - turning away from an addiction,
  - being reconciled with our family,
  - forgiving an old hurt,
  - going to confession after a long absence.
Once we are there we look back and wonder at our resistance.
Here was something that we needed in order to live,

and yet we did not recognise it;
the truth of ourselves demanded it,
and yet we did not accept to do it.
Now, Lord, by your grace,
we know that your Word has been made flesh
and found a home in us. Thank you, Lord.

'One of the deepest joys of life is to be used for a purpose recognised by yourself as a mighty one.' George Bernard Shaw
Lord, we thank you for times
when we have the deep satisfaction of knowing
that we were working for a noble cause,
one that we know is far greater than ourselves,
even though we are making a contribution to it,
so that we can say like John the Baptist that what comes after us
ranks before us because it existed before us.

'There is nothing in my former ministry that I would repudiate except my many sins and shortcomings. My becoming a priest in the Roman Catholic Church will be the completion and right ordering of what was begun thirty years ago.' Richard Neuhaus, Lutheran pastor, on entering the Catholic Church and asking for ordination as a priest; October 1990
Lord, we pray for all those
who are becoming members of our church,
that they may experience their life up to now as being fulfilled,
as having received from your fullness,
the grace of the present fulfilling the grace of the past.

The Epiphany of the Lord

Gospel reading: Matthew 2:1-12

[1]*After Jesus had been born at Bethlehem in Judaea during the reign of King Herod, some wise men came to Jerusalem from the east.* [2]*'Where is the infant king of the Jews?' they asked. 'We saw his star as it rose and have come to do him homage.'*

[3]*When King Herod heard this he was perturbed, and so was the whole of Jerusalem.* [4]*He called together all the chief priests and the scribes of the people, and enquired of them where the Christ was to be born.* [5]*'At Bethlehem in Judaea,' they told him, 'for this is what the prophet wrote:* [6]*And you, Bethlehem, in the land of Judaea, you are by no means least among the leaders of Judah, for out of you will come a leader who will shepherd my people Israel.'* [7]*Then Herod summoned the wise men to see him privately. He asked them the exact date on which the star had appeared,* [8]*and sent them on to Bethlehem. 'Go and find out all about the child,' he said, 'and when you have found him, let me know, so that I too may go and do him homage.'*

[9]*Having listened to what the king had to say, they set out. And there in front of them was the star they had seen rising; it went forward and halted over the place where the child was.* [10]*The sight of the star filled them with delight,* [11]*and going into the house they saw the child with his mother Mary, and falling to their knees they did him homage. Then, opening their treasures, they offered him gifts of gold and frankincense and myrrh.*

[12]*But they were warned in a dream not to go back to Herod, and returned to their own country by a different way.*

In the Christmas story as told by St Luke, the Word made flesh manifests himself to the shepherds; in St Matthew's version, he manifests himself to the wise men from the East. Although at first sight the two stories seem different, they are in fact basically alike – as you will discover when you meditate on each passage – since there is only one God and he has one way of relating with us.

For this feast, then, make the journey with the wise men, as you did with the shepherds on Christmas Day and on January 1st.

The story is told in clearly defined stages, and you will find that each of these stages will touch you in your meditation, so that you need not include the entire story in order to do a good meditation.

Verses 1 and 2 tell us of the journey from 'the east' to Jerusalem, and the symbolism of the first searching which takes us some of the way, before we get lost and have to resort to a religious centre.

In verses 3 to 9 we have the meeting between the wise men and Herod – very dramatic, and so true to experience. You can read these verses from the point of view of the wise men, so humble and open to learning from religious leaders, even though these have bad motives; or from the point of view of Herod, typical of ourselves when we are in a position of authority and privilege and become insecure at the mere thought of a new religious insight.

In verses 10 and 11 we have the touching story of all moments of grace – the joy of recognition, the sense of homecoming, the simplicity of the presence of God. The mention of the 'treasures' is clearly meant to convey the arrival of other cultures doing homage to Jesus.

Verse 12 is very significant, indicating the new-found freedom of the believers.

* * *

Lord, there comes a point in our lives when we finally discover what we want to give our whole lives to:
    - a cause like racial equality, community development,
    women's rights;
    - a spirituality which combines union with God and social
    involvement;
    - the religious life or the priesthood;
    - contemplative prayer.
We look back on the long journey that brought us to this point,
from the time we knew in some vague way
that we wanted to change our ways
– like the wise men seeing a star as it rose
and deciding to follow it.
Then, as it always seems to happen on a spiritual journey,
we lost sight of the star and drifted aimlessly for some years,
until we realised that the only sensible thing to do

was to get help.
So we went to our religious leaders,
and though they were rather confused themselves,
they put us back on the right track
and the old enthusiasm returned.
The last part of the journey went quickly:
suddenly we knew that we had found
what we had been looking for,
and it was like coming home, so that we went into the house,
fell on our knees and opened our treasures.
Thank you, Lord, for guiding us every part of the way.

Lord, it is strange how we become attached
to positions of privilege
   - as parents or teachers;
   - occupying a position in the church;
   - accepted as one of the better educated members of our little
     circle.
When people come forward
who are from a different background,
or who are asking new questions,
we are pertubed,
as Herod was when the wise men came to Jerusalem.
We reflect on what to say, and may even give them good advice,
but deep down our main concern is
that we should continue to feel secure where we are.
No wonder those whom we help do not come back to us
but return to their country by a different way.

Lord, for many centuries now the church has been European.
We thank you that in our day
people of other cultures are looking for Jesus
because they have seen a star out in the east.
Naturally, we are perturbed by all these foreigners,
and so is the whole of Jerusalem,
for they will bring changes to the whole church,
and we will lose our special status.
So, though we give them the right instructions,
we tell them that once they have discovered Jesus

they must come back and tell us exactly what they have found.
But you are guiding them, Lord, and when they come to Jesus
they will open the treasures of their own cultures.
Furthermore, you will reveal to them
that there is no need to come back to us,
and they will make their own way home.

Lord, we sometimes think that we must spend plenty of money
to make Jesus more attractive, or that we must be very learned
so that our preaching of him can draw many to him.
But wise men are looking for an infant king,
and the scriptures say that he will come from Bethlehem,
the least among the leaders of Judah,
because people are tired of great kings who dominate them.
But if they go into a simple house
and see the child Jesus with his mother Mary,
even as they fall on their knees and do him homage
they will feel comfortable to open their treasures
and offer him gifts of gold, frankincense and myrrh.

Lord, we look today for instant results
and for the 'quick fix' in all things,
so that we end up looking for instant spiritual growth as well.
But before we can see Jesus
and fall on our knees and do him homage
we have to make a long journey from the east.
We have to follow a star,
lose it and discover it again many times,
until finally it halts over the place where he is.

The Baptism of the Lord

Gospel reading: Luke 3:15-16; 21-22

15*A feeling of expectancy had grown among the people, who were be-ginning to think that John might be the Christ,* 16*so John declared before them all, 'I baptise you with water, but someone is coming, someone who is more powerful than I am, and I am not fit to undo the strap of his sandals; he will baptise you with the Holy Spirit and fire.*
21*Now when all the people had been baptised and while Jesus after his own baptism was at prayer, heaven opened* 22*and the Holy Spirit de-scended on him in bodily shape, like a dove. And a voice came from heaven, 'You are my Son, the Beloved; my favour rests on you.'*

The Baptism of the Lord is told in all four gospels with each one giving its own slant. We must be faithful to the text before us – St Luke's version.

The story can be read from different perspectives; in our meditation we are free to choose the one which corresponds best to our experience.
- It is first of all an extraordinary religious experience. St Luke's is the only version which says that Jesus 'was at prayer'. Luke does not emphasise the actual baptism at all, but presents it as the prelude to the main event – the descent of the Holy Spirit and the voice from heaven.

We should enter fully into the images:
  - 'Heaven opened' indicates that all dualism is broken down – between God and humanity, between humanity and na-ture.
  - 'The Holy Spirit descended in bodily shape, like a dove' – the experience of the Holy Spirit is vivid but very gentle.
  - 'A voice came from heaven' should be interpreted in the same spirit as the coming of the Holy Spirit. It is so vivid and so gentle that it could only have come from heaven.

The voice makes three statements, each with its own impor-tance:
  - 'You are my son' – in the Bible, divine sonship is attributed to kings, usually on the occasion of their enthronement; royal power is conferred on Jesus.

- 'The beloved' – Jesus is assured that he is loved tenderly, as a bridegroom is loved by his bride.
- 'My favour rests on you' says that God's love remains permanently with him – it is not something temporary. We are reminded of Jesus' words at the Last Supper, 'As the Father has loved me so I have loved you, remain in my love' (Jn 5:9).
- Verses 21 and 22 make no reference to the historical context, but the inclusion of verses 15 and 16 in the liturgical reading reminds us that Jesus' baptism took place when John the Baptist's ministry was about to come to an end. The baptism was therefore Jesus' call to public ministry. This fits the biblical pattern by which a call to do God's work is always preceded by a deep experience of God, e.g. Isaiah, Jeremiah, Gideon in the Old Testament, Mary and Zechariah in the New.

  Experience bears out that this pattern of a deep personal experience leading to a new commitment occurs in the lives of many people. It happened to saints such as Augustine, Ignatius of Loyola, Teresa of Avila and Margaret Mary, and to many other great men and women. We can identify a similar pattern in our own lives too.
- Even though, as noted above, St Luke downplays Jesus' baptism, we are free to focus on it. St Luke notes that Jesus came forward 'when all the people had been baptised,' inviting us to see him as entering into solidarity with those who had come to John for baptism.
- In St Luke's version, Jesus' baptism was a personal experience. It happened when he was 'at prayer' and 'the voice which came from heaven' was addressed to him -- 'You are...'. This interpretation is not insisted on, however, so we have the latitude to interpret the story as a proclamation to the bystanders. It then becomes the story of when we perceive the spark of divinity in someone we previously looked down on.

* * *

*'In discovering the Father, Jesus has found an 'other' ('I and the Father
are one'); in the Spirit he has discovered his non-duality with Yahweh.'*
Abhishiktanda (Dom Henri Le Saulx)

Lord, we thank you
for deep prayer experiences when we are truly one with Jesus.
They always come to us as your free gift, unexpectedly,
after a long time of struggle when we felt we were drowning,
abandoned by all, including you.
After we have been baptised in these waters of loneliness,
suddenly
     - heaven opens and we feel at one with the universe,
      the sun, the moon and the stars all seem close;
     - your Holy Spirit descends on us,
     his powerful but gentle presence so vivid
     that it is almost in a bodily shape like a dove;
     - we hear a voice resonating so deeply within us
     we know it must come from heaven,
     - telling us that we are not aliens in the world
     but princes and princesses,
     members of your royal family,
     - that we are beloved,
     - and we must never allow ourselves to feel abandoned
     since your favour rests forever on us.
Thank you, Lord.

Lord, remind us that we do not dare enter your presence
except we are in communion with the rest of humanity,
and especially with the humblest of our brothers and sisters,
     - those written off as sinners by our church community;
     - the victims of racism, sexism, elitism and religious
     persecution;
     - abandoned by their families because they are HIV positive;
     - those who are mentally or physically handicapped.
It is only when, like Jesus,
we have had our own baptism of solidarity with them
that we can enter confidently into prayer,
     - look for the heavens to be opened,
     - your Holy Spirit to descend on us
     in bodily shape like a dove,

- your voice to assure us
that we are your Sons and Daughters, your beloved,
and that your favour rests on us.

*'The more a Christian community is rooted in the experience of God,
the more credibly it will be able to proclaim to others the fulfillment of
God's Kingdom in Jesus Christ.'* Ecclesia in Asia
Lord, before we embark on a new direction in our lives
   - the religious life, or marriage,
    - a political involvement,
   - going to a foreign country to improve ourselves,
   - giving up a secure job so that we can serve the poor,
teach us to first humble ourselves before you, as Jesus did.
Only after we have been baptised will the heavens be opened,
the Spirit descend on us in bodily shape, like a dove,
and your voice will proclaim that we are your Beloved
and your favour rests on us.
Then, like Jesus, we will be ready to commit ourselves
to the new venture you have called us to.

Lord, forgive us that as a church we tend to come to others
with feelings of superiority.
Help us rather to see your son Jesus in whatever culture,
ethnic group, race or social class you invite us to enter.
The world may describe them
as backward, primitive, third world, unemployable or lazy;
we pray that we will stand before them with respect
until we see the heavens opened
and the Holy Spirit descending on them,
gently like a dove, and hear your voice proclaiming mightily
that these are your Sons and Daughters, your Beloved,
and that your favour rests on them.

First Sunday of Lent

Gospel reading: Luke 4:1-13

[1]*Filled with the Holy Spirit, Jesus left the Jordan and was led by the Spirit through the wilderness,* [2]*being tempted there by the devil for forty days. During that time he ate nothing and at the end he was hungry.* [3]*Then the devil said to him, 'If you are the Son of God, tell this stone to turn into a loaf.'* [4]*But Jesus replied, 'Scripture says, "Man does not live on bread alone".'* [5]*Then leading him to a height, the devil showed him in a moment of time all the kingdoms of the world and said to him,* [6]*'I will give you all this power and the glory of these kingdoms, for it has been committed to me and I give it to anyone I choose.* [7]*Worship me, then, and it shall all be yours.'* [8]*But Jesus answered him, 'Scripture says, "You must worship the Lord your God, and serve him alone."'* [9]*Then he led him to Jerusalem and made him stand on the parapet of the Temple. 'If you are the Son of God,' he said to him 'throw yourself down from here,* [10]*for scripture says, "He will put his angels in charge of you to guard you," and again:* [11]*"they will hold you up on their hands in case you hurt your foot against a stone."'* [12]*But Jesus answered him, 'It has been said, "You must not put the Lord your God to the test."'* [13]*Having exhausted all these ways of tempting him, the devil left him, to return at the appointed time.*

The story of Jesus' temptation reveals to us the deepest thing about him: he had total trust in his heavenly Father. This is why the incident is placed at the very beginning of his public life. The evangelists are telling us that he chose this path and he would remain faithful to it through all the ups and downs of his ministry.

Telling the story in the form of 'temptations' does two things:
- Jesus' attitude is highlighted since it is set in contrast with other possible attitudes;
- we are reminded that for Jesus trust was a free and deliberate choice, as it is for every human being: he chose to trust.

In meditating on the temptations, feel free to focus on the one that appeals to you and remain with it until you find yourself identifying deeply with it. Eventually you will find that all three are really variations on the one temptation not to be totally trusting.

The story has an introduction in verses 1 and 2 and a conclusion in verse 13. You might like to spend some time on these verses as they are very significant.

* * *

'What use are victories on the battlefields if we are defeated in our innermost personal selves?' Maximillian Kolbe

Lord, we like to remain on the banks of the river Jordan
where we busy ourselves with external activities,
organizing communities, entering into relationships,
academic discussions.
We pray that during these forty days of Lent
we may allow ourselves to be led by the Holy Spirit
into the depths of ourselves,
into the wilderness, away from the world of achievements,
where we can face up to the evil tendencies
that are active within us:
> - our feeling that as children of God we have the right to dominate the world as we will;
> - our yearning for the power and the glory of earthly kingdoms;
> - the subtle ways in which we try to manipulate you.

We need not be afraid of this wilderness experience, Lord,
because even if we have to face evil in ourselves,
we will also discover, like Jesus,
that trust in your love is a law written deep within us,
and when the devil has exhausted all these ways of tempting us
he will leave.
But, Lord, do not let us become complacent,
because he will return at some time you have appointed,
and we must be ready to start the struggle all over again.

Lord, as a church,
we are inclined to remain on the banks of the Jordan,
content to baptise and preach and look after our church affairs.
But if, like Jesus, we are filled with your Holy Spirit,
we too will leave the Jordan
and let the Spirit lead us through the wilderness,
through the worlds of politics, business,

industrial relations and international trade,
being tempted there by the devil as all our contemporaries are,
so that we can find even within those wildernesses
that the words of scripture are still true.

Lord, we remember today a difficult period in our lives:
    - our financial situation was very precarious;
    - we had a succession of failures in our work;
    - our children were causing us problems.
You led us through the wilderness for those forty days;
we felt as if we had nothing to nourish ourselves
and we were hungry.
We were resentful too: were we not the children of God?
Why could we not take up a stone
and tell it to turn into a loaf of bread?
Then one day it suddenly came home to us
that there is much more to life than having our needs satisfied.
We had discovered that we had loyal friends, good health,
and most of all trust in you.
Jesus had reminded us how scripture says that man does not
live on bread alone.

'The hope that rests on calculation has lost its innocence.' Thomas Merton
Lord, in the world today, people like to plan things rationally
and we would like to plan our lives that way too.
We would like to go up on a height
and see in a moment of time all the kingdoms of this world,
and then find out to whom the power and the glory
of these kingdoms have been committed
so that they can be given to us.
But that, Lord, is the way of calculation,
whereas to become whole persons
we must take the way of Jesus,
which is to have as our only security that we worship you,
our Lord and God, and that we serve you alone.

Lord, we thank you
for great people who have touched our lives,
not world figures or those who make the headlines,
but ordinary people who have done their duty without fuss:
- parents who brought up handicapped children;
- dedicated teachers;
- business people who remained honest.
We thank you that they knew how to remain in the wilderness,
not threatening to throw themselves
from the parapet of the temple
and calling on you to send angels
who would guard them and hold them in their hands
so that they would not hurt their feet against a stone.
Like Jesus, they knew that you were their Lord and God,
and they did not have to put your love to the test.

Lord, Lent is a time when we have deep prayer experiences,
and we might think that in those experiences
we are free from the evil one.
Remind us, Lord, that there is a temptation
special to those who stand at the parapet of your temple,
and that is to become arrogant towards you,
to insist that your angels must hold us up
in case we hurt our feet against a stone.
Help us, Lord, in our prayers,
to remain perfectly still and trusting,
remembering, like Jesus, how it is said
that we must not put you, our Lord and God, to the test.

Second Sunday of Lent

Gospel reading: Luke 9:28-36

28Jesus took with him Peter and John and James and went up the mountain to pray. 29As he prayed, the aspect of his face was changed and his clothing became brilliant as lightning. 30Suddenly, there were two men there talking to him; they were Moses and Elijah 31appearing in glory, and they were speaking of his passing, which he was to accomplish in Jerusalem. 32Peter and his companions were heavy with sleep, but they kept awake and saw his glory and the two men standing with him.

33As these were leaving him, Peter said to Jesus, 'Master, it is wonderful for us to be here; so let us make three tents, one for you, one for Moses and one for Elijah.' He did not know what he was saying.

34As he spoke, a cloud came and covered them with shadow; and when they went into the cloud, the disciples were afraid. 35And a voice came from the cloud, saying: 'This is my Son, the Chosen One. Listen to him.' 36And after the voice had spoken, Jesus was found alone. The disciples kept silence and, at that time, told no one what they had seen.

Though we usually refer to this incident as the Transfiguration, Jesus' appearing in glory was only the first stage of the experience the apostles had with him on the mountain. In your meditation then, feel free to enter the story at any stage, and even to remain with any part of the story that touches you, although you might also want to identify with the entire experience taken as a whole.

In verse 28, Jesus takes his three followers up the mountain to pray, and this is a symbol of the withdrawal that must take place before he can be transfigured.

In verses 29 to 31 the transfiguration is described as something that happened to Jesus himself first, before it was seen by the apostles. Note two points that are specific to St Luke's account:

- the change happens while he is praying;
- Moses and Elijah were speaking to him about his passion.

Verses 32 and 33 give us Peter's response. St Luke stresses that it was because he saw them leaving that he wanted to make the tents.

In verses 34 and 35 we have a sharp contrast: the apostles who were covered by a cloud, now experience the glory of Jesus, not visibly but through a heavenly voice.

Verse 36 is a brief and sober conclusion to the episode.

* * *

Lord, commitment to a noble cause involves a long and painful journey:
- to practice non-violence in all our relationships;
- to work for social transformation according to gospel values;
- to live the evangelical counsels.

There is a first glorious moment
when we are led by our leader up a mountain
– aspects are changed
and ordinary garments become brilliant as lightning;
suddenly our great predecessors are with us
and they are talking to us about the great victory
that will soon come to pass.
It is wonderful for us to be there,
and we want to make tents for ourselves.
But we do not know what we are saying,
because the words are barely out of our mouths
when a cloud comes and covers us with its shadow
– obstacles arise, we start to quarrel among ourselves,
and some drop out.
We feel a terrible fear as we go into the cloud,
but we need not be afraid
because within that cloud we find our commitment.
It is as if from the cloud a voice comes from heaven
assuring us that we have perceived a personal call from God,
and we must follow it.
From that moment on, we know that we can stand alone,
and we feel no need to tell others what we have seen,
because we no longer need their approval.

Lord, we who are leaders of communities, of families, of parishes,
or the country,
we spend too much time and effort talking about love, respect
and loyalty.

Teach us to do like Jesus, to take our community with us
and go up the mountain to pray together,
so that as we pray we may see the glory that is within us.
Our aspects will appear changed
and outer appearances which seemed shabby
will become brilliant as lightning.
Then suddenly we will become aware
that we are in communion with our ancestors
and we are preparing ourselves for the crises
that we are about to face.

Lord, we remember today all those
who will be attending parish missions during the coming week.
Often, they will come heavy with sleep
and burdened with worries;
we pray that they may keep awake and see the glory of Jesus
and all the saints standing with him, so that they will say to him,
'Master, it is wonderful for us to be here.'

*'Prayer means yearning for the simple presence of God, for a personal
understanding of his word, for knowledge of his will and for capacity to
hear and obey him.'* Thomas Merton
Lord, help us not to be content in our prayer
with glorious visions
which make us feel wonderful to be there.
Teach us rather to yearn for deeper prayer,
for your cloud to come and cover us with shadow
while we enter into it, fearful and trembling,
and then, for your voice to come from that dark cloud,
as we remain totally silent
and experience that we must listen
to the precious word you have spoken.

Lord, in our modern world,
we have lost the art of listening to people.
Teach us to wait for another with reverence,
putting aside our prejudices,
our personal plans and expectations,
as if a cloud has come and covered us with shadow,

and we have gone into the cloud with utter poverty,
knowing only that we must listen to this precious child of God
whom he has chosen out of all humanity
to stand before us at this moment.

Lord, we thank you for deep experiences:
    - moments of intimacy between spouses;
    - an insight that changed our whole way of thinking;
    - the times we feel at one with ourselves and with all creation.
After such experiences, we are like the three disciples
– we keep silence and can tell no one what we have seen.

'Before I understood prayer, the mountains were nothing but mountains, and the rivers were nothing but rivers. When I got into prayer, the mountains were no longer mountains, and the rivers no longer rivers. But when I understood prayer, the mountains were only mountains, and the rivers only rivers.' Zen saying
Lord, take us along that journey
by which Jesus takes us with him up the mountain
and we see glory; then we hear your voice
saying he is your Son, the Chosen One,
and then after the voice has spoken he is found alone with us.

Third Sunday of Lent

Gospel reading: Luke 13:1-9

¹*It was about this time that some people arrived and told Jesus about the Galileans whose blood Pilate had mingled with that of their sacrifices.* ²*At this he said to them, 'Do you suppose these Galileans who suffered like that were greater sinners than any other Galileans?* ³*They were not, I tell you. No; but unless you repent you will all perish as they did.* ⁴*Or those eighteen on whom the tower at Siloam fell and killed them? Do you suppose that they were more guilty than all the other people living in Jerusalem?* ⁵*They were not, I tell you. No; but unless you repent you will all perish as they did.'*

⁶*He told this parable: 'A man had a fig tree planted in his vineyard, and he came looking for fruit on it but found none.* ⁷*He said to the man who looked after the vineyard, "Look here, for three years now I have been coming to look for fruit on this fig tree and finding none. Cut it down: why should it be taking up the ground?"* ⁸*"Sir," the man replied, "leave it one more year and give me time to dig round it and manure it:* ⁹*it may bear fruit next year; if not, then you can cut it down".'*

Verses 1 to 5 are in two groups – 1 to 3 and then 4 to 5; they are practically identical, so that reading them together has a cumulative effect on us. Each is based on a tragic incident: Pilate murdering a group of Galileans as they were offering sacrifice in the temple, and a tower falling and killing eighteen people.

You can start your meditation by identifying a moment when you learnt of (or saw on television) a tragedy where there was violence and bloodshed. The tower was probably a religious building, so that both incidents took place in a religious setting. Then identify with the two possible responses: that of the people, and that taught by Jesus. Note the forceful way in which he rejects the first response. Ask yourself when you have experienced that kind of challenge to what was a natural and spontaneous response.

In verses 6 to 9 we have a parable. Interpret it with your feelings. Here again, start with a moment, a time when you or someone else, or a community, had a terrible feeling of uselessness; then identify with the two possible responses, that of the owner,

on the one hand, and that of the one who looked after the vineyard, on the other. The designation of one as 'owner' and the
other as 'looking after' is of course highly significant, and the
parable is meant to evoke for us a moment of grace, when we experienced the love of God.

* * *

Lord, there is violence in many countries today: we think of Iraq,
Northern Ireland, Algeria, Sri Lanka, the Holy Land.
When we see scenes of violence in those countries
on our television screens,
we naturally suppose that people there
are greater sinners than we are.
Preserve us, Lord, from that kind of complacency;
send us some Jesus person to tell us that it is not so,
by any means;
that we too do not respect those
whose politics are different from ours;
we too have our racism and our religious intolerance,
and if we do not repent,
we will perish as people in those countries are perishing.

Lord, even when we help others,
we like to do it from a position of superiority.
We label them 'those in need' or 'poor sinners'
or 'those less fortunate than ourselves,'
as if they belong to a different breed of people.
Every once in a while, however, you pull us up short:
    - we find that we too are sinners;
    - someone from a different faith corrects us;
    - a person we thought we were helping turns out not to need
    our help at all.
We feel embarrassed and humiliated,
but that is Jesus reprimanding us because we supposed
that those we were helping were greater sinners than any of us,
whereas we were just as much
in need of repentance as they were.

'The hour for action has sounded. At stake are the peace of the world and the future of civilisation. It is time for all men and all peoples to face up to their responsibilities.' Pope Paul VI, *Populorum progressio*

Lord, we thank you
that recent popes have been speaking with the voice of Jesus,
challenging us to stop looking at violence
as something that happens to individuals because of their sins,
and see it rather as something
that has its roots in our civilisation,
in particular in our lack of moral principles
and our individualism;
and unless we repent, we will all perish.

Lord, there was a time when we felt very vulnerable:
    - one of our children had let us down;
    - we were without a job;
    - we realised that we were getting old.
We felt useless,
as if someone had come to look at us looking for fruit,
and had found none;
as if we were merely taking up ground,
and the only thing we deserved
was to be cut down and thrown away.
We thank you, Lord, that at such moments you send us friends,
not wishy-washy people who flatter us
and pretend that we are without blame,
but real friends like Jesus:
they tell us that indeed we deserve to be cut down,
but that it is not too late, and we can still bear fruit in the future,
and they promise to care for us
and help us so that we can make a new start.

Lord, there are people in authority
who look on members of their communities
purely as producers,
and are impatient when they do not get results from them.
We find people like that in government, in the church,
and even among parents and teachers.
They are like landowners

who have planted trees on their property
and when they come looking for fruit for three years
and find none,
they get angry and want to cut down the trees
as useless and only taking up ground.
But we thank you, Lord, for those who are different,
who are like you, who have a feel for people
and know that someone who has borne no fruit for many years
could still do so in the future;
they are always ready to try again with people,
trusting that with more care and attention
they might bear fruit next year.

Lord, in the world today, when something doesn't work,
we throw it away and get a new one.
We pray for those who work the land
and who have learnt patience from it.
They know, for example, that trees are precious
and must not be cut down except as a very last resort,
so that they are always willing to take time
to dig around them and manure them,
in case they might still be capable of bearing fruit;
in this way they are a parable of your love for us,
and of how you want us to treat one another.

Lord, when we think of nuclear war hanging over us,
we feel as if you have given humanity one more year,
to see if we will bear fruit and if not then we will be cut down.

Fourth Sunday of Lent

Gospel reading: Luke 15:1-3;11-32

¹*The tax collectors and the sinners, meanwhile, were all seeking the company of Jesus to hear what he had to say,* ²*and the Pharisees and the Scribes complained. 'This man,' they said, 'welcomes sinners and eats with them.'* ³ *So he spoke this parable to them:*

¹¹*A man had two sons.* ¹²*The younger said to his father, 'Father, let me have the share of the estate that would come to me.' So the father divided the property between them.* ¹³*A few days later, the younger son got together everything he had and left for a distant country, where he squandered his money on a life of debauchery.*

¹⁴*When he had spent it all, that country experienced a severe famine, and now he began to feel the pinch,* ¹⁵*so he hired himself out to one of the local inhabitants who put him on his farm to feed the pigs.* ¹⁶*And he would willingly have filled his belly with the husks the pigs were eating, but no one offered him anything.*

¹⁷*Then he came to his senses and said, 'How many of my father's servants have more food than they want, and here I am dying of hunger!* ¹⁸*I will leave this place and go to my father and say: 'Father, I have sinned against heaven and against you;* ¹⁹*I no longer deserve to be called your son; treat me as one of your paid servants.'*

²⁰*So he left the place and went back to his father. While he was still a long way off, his father saw him and was moved with pity. He ran to the boy, clasped him in his arms and kissed him tenderly.* ²¹*Then his son said, 'Father, I have sinned against heaven and against you. I no longer deserve to be called your son.'* ²²*But the father said to his servants, 'Quick! Bring out the best robe and put it on him; put a ring on his finger and sandals on his feet.* ²³*Bring the calf we have been fattening, and kill it; we are going to have a feast, a celebration,* ²⁴*because this son of mine was dead and has come back to life; he was lost and is found.' And they began to celebrate.*

²⁵*Now the elder son was in the fields, and on his way back, as he drew near the house, he could hear music and dancing.* ²⁶*Calling one of the servants, he asked what it was all about.* ²⁷*'Your brother has come,' replied the servant, 'and your father has killed the calf we had fattened because he has got him back safe and sound.'*

²⁸*He was angry then and refused to go in, and his father came out to*

plead with him; [29]*but he answered his father, 'Look, all these years I have slaved for you and never once disobeyed your orders, yet you never offered me so much as a kid for me to celebrate with my friends.* [30]*But, for this son of yours, when he comes back after swallowing up your property – he and his women – you kill the calf you had been fattening.'* [31]*The father said, 'My son, you are with me always and all I have is yours.* [32]*But it was only right we should celebrate and rejoice, because your brother here was dead and has come to life; he was lost and is found.''*

Verses 1 to 3 are one of several passages in the gospels which give us an overall picture of Jesus' lifestyle. In your meditation, identify who for you are 'the tax collectors and sinners,' people who are outsiders to the community; then, who is Jesus, and finally, who are 'the Pharisees and Scribes' who complain.

The main part of the passage is, of course, the parable of the Prodigal Son, one of the most touching passages in the whole Bible, and indeed of all religious literature. It is also the longest parable in the gospels, and so you will have to concentrate on one section of it.

Though it is usually called the parable of the Prodigal Son, it really speaks of three people, and we can meditate profitably on each of them.

The father is the symbol of the perfect lover: you can see him at three points in the story:
- in verse 12, when the younger son asks for his share of the property;
- in verses 20 to 24, when the younger son returns;
- in verses 31 to 32, when he goes out to the older son.

The story of the younger son is in four stages:
- his original choice in verses 11 and 12;
- the result of this choice in verses 14 to 16;
- his first and flawed movement of repentance in verses 17 to 20;
- his return home in verses 20 to 24.

Don't neglect the older son. His story too is very significant for us, and especially for us religious people. His basic attitude is in verses 25 to 30, and when he meets his father in verses 31 to 32.

* * *

Lord, every church community, without realising it,
gradually becomes an exclusive group,
where we speak a language that only we understand
and whole categories of people feel uncomfortable;
but you always send Jesus to open up the community.
One such person was Pope John XXIII.
We remember how every kind of person sought his company
and wanted to hear what he had to say,
and he in turn welcomed them and ate with them.
Some in the church complained, but the world was grateful
because they recognised that Jesus was present among them.

*'We must build a world where freedom is not an empty word and where
the poor man, Lazarus, can sit down at the same table with the rich
man.'* Pope Paul VI
Lord, there is famine in the world today:
  - workers having to hire themselves out to work in foreign
    countries, doing menial tasks;
  - children willing to fill their bellies with food fit only for an-
    imals, and no one gives them anything.
Lord, help us to retrace our steps,
to recognise the root cause of our problems,
that individualism by which children of the one father
want to have the share of the estate for themselves alone,
and once they have collected what they see as theirs,
leave for a far distant country.
Lord, bring us back to understand the world
as our father's house:
  - where the word 'hired servant' is not mentioned;
  - where we are always with one another;
  - where when one is lost all feel pain, and when one who was
    lost is found, all rejoice.

Lord, we remember parents today.
How often they must go along with children
who want to take what is their due
and cannot intervene when those most dear to them leave
for a distant country
where they squander their money on a life of debauchery.

They must wait until their children come to their senses
and decide to leave that place and return.
Teach them, Lord, that you too have had that experience.

Lord, we thank you for people who have taught us
what true forgiveness is
– spouses, parents, faithful friends, a parish community.
We thought forgiveness meant
having to say to the one we had offended,
'I have sinned against heaven and against you,'
and being treated as a hired servant rather than as family.
We know now that forgiveness is something totally different,
it is seeing the one who offended us from a long way off,
running to him, and clasping him in our arms,
and kissing him tenderly,
bringing our best robe to put on him,
putting a ring on his finger and sandals on his feet
and having a feast, a celebration,
because one who was dead has come back to life
and one who was lost is found.

Lord, we pray today for those who are facing death
and who are afraid,
that they may find peace
in the confidence that when they die they go home,
and you will run to meet them,
will clasp them in your arms and kiss them tenderly,
angels will bring out the best robe and put it on them;
they will have died, but have entered into life,
have been lost for a while, but are now found forever.

*'We are not on earth as museum keepers, but to cultivate a flourishing
garden of life, and to prepare a glorious future.'* Pope John XXIII
Lord, many people spend their time complaining,
complaining that they have worked hard
and not got their due reward,
or that others have wasted time and money
and have been blessed.
We see this even in the church.

We thank you for people like Mother Teresa
who enlarge our horizons
and show us how petty our concerns are,
who open up for us new possibilities in human relationships,
where one person can say to another,
'I am always with you,' and 'all I have is yours.'

*'It is God who demands that man should be free; man himself loves
servitude and easily comes to terms with it.'* Berdyaev
Set us free from our bondage, Lord,
showing us that you are always with us and all you have is ours.

Fifth Sunday of Lent

Gospel reading: John 8:1-11

1Jesus went to the Mount of Olives. 2At daybreak, he appeared in the Temple again; and as all the people came to him, he sat down and began to teach them.

3The scribes and Pharisees brought a woman along who had been caught committing adultery; and making her stand there in full view of everybody, 4they said to Jesus, 'Master, this woman was caught in the very act of committing adultery, 5and Moses has ordered us in the Law to condemn women like this to death by stoning. What have you to say?'

6They asked him this as a test, looking for something to use against him. But Jesus bent down and started writing on the ground with his finger. 7As they persisted with their question, he looked up and said, 'If there is one of you who has not sinned, let him be the first to throw a stone at her.' 8Then he bent down and wrote on the ground again.

9When they heard this, they went away one by one, beginning with the eldest, until Jesus was left alone with the woman, who remained standing there. 10He looked up and said, 'Woman, where are they? Has no one condemned you?' 11'No one, sir,' she replied. 'Neither do I condemn you,' said Jesus, 'Go your way, and do not sin any more.'

There are three people in today's passage:
- the woman;
- the group called 'scribes and Pharisees';
- Jesus.

As always, in your meditation you must let yourself enter the story from the viewpoint of one of the three.

- The woman was guilty of a sexual sin, but her story evokes any experience of having done something shameful in a moment of great vulnerability.

- The scribes and Pharisees are typical of powerful people who have no feeling for the weak. There are several things about them that might touch you: that they have singled out this one sin for condemnation; that they are using the woman to score points against Jesus; or that they use pious phrases to mask their cruelty – all types of behaviour that are easily recognisable.

- This picture of Jesus is one of the most touching in the gospels; look at his action of bending down and writing on the ground. It suggests tremendous inner strength which, in a non-violent way, unmasks the hypocrisy of the accusers.

* * *

'Those who live in constant terror of their own sins are powerless to ac-complish anything in the world.' Berdyaev
Lord,
there was a time when the feeling of guilt had us paralysed.
We felt condemned by voices within us:
   - sermons we had heard in our childhood threatening us with hell fire;
   - teachers who told us we had to be perfect.
We felt as if we were standing in full view of our accusers
and they were condemning us as deserving of death.
We thank you, Lord, that you sent us, at that moment,
a wise and kind person, who stayed with us, saying nothing,
just being there like Jesus bent down and writing on the ground,
until, very gradually, as the weeks went by,
the harsh accusing voices were silenced, one by one,
beginning from the most deeply rooted,
and eventually we were standing there
knowing you were looking at us,
and telling us that we were now free to go out
and lead a good and creative life.

'All condemnation is of the devil. We condemn others only because we shun condemning ourselves.' St Seraphim of Sarov
Lord, we who are community leaders
in the church or the country
often have to point out people's faults.
Help us to do so without condemning them.
But that is not easy; we have to listen to our innermost selves,
waiting patiently until every scribe and Pharisee within us
has walked away
because only then do we have the right to look at another
and say, 'Go, and sin no more.'

Lord, just as in the time of Jesus,
society pronounces its harshest judgments
on those who are caught committing sexual sins,
especially if they are women.
Authorities will always single them out
and make them stand in full view of everybody,
insisting that in the name of religion
they must condemn such persons to death by stoning.
We pray, Lord, that your church will be like Jesus,
pointing out the hypocrisy of the accusers,
and protecting the dignity of those who have sinned.

*'One form of gentleness we should practice is towards ourselves. It is
reasonable to be displeased and sorry when we commit faults, but not
fretful or spiteful to ourselves.'* St Francis de Sales
Lord, teach us to look at ourselves with respect and compassion,
as Jesus looked at the woman taken in adultery
when he was left alone with her
and she remained standing before him.

Lord, send us leaders like Jesus,
who will stand with the weak and the vulnerable
against their oppressors,
not aggressively, but calmly,
so that the oppressors walk away of their own accord,
and the weak find the space to create a good life for themselves.

Lord, we remember a time when we were
using a Bible passage to condemn someone,
and quite suddenly the passage came alive for us,
and we saw that we were condemning the other
for what we were guilty of ourselves,
so that we let the stone fall from our hands and went our way.

Palm Sunday

Gospel reading: Luke 19:28-40

28Jesus went on ahead, going up to Jerusalem. 29Now when he was near Bethphage, close by the Mount of Olives, as it is called, he sent two of the disciples, telling them, 30'Go off to the village opposite, and as you enter it you will find a tethered colt that no one has yet ridden. Untie it and bring it here. 31If anyone asks you, "Why are you untying it?" you are to say this, "The Master needs it."' 32The messengers went off and found everything just as he had told them. 33As they were untying the colt, its owner said, 'Why are you untying that colt?' 34and they answered, 'The Master needs it.' 35So they took the colt to Jesus, and throwing their garments over its back, they helped Jesus onto it. 36As he moved off, people spread their cloaks in the road, and now, as he was approaching the downward slope of the Mount of Olives, 37the whole group of disciples joyfully began to praise God at the top of their voices for all the miracles they had seen. 38They cried out:

'Blessings on the King who comes,
in the name of the Lord!
Peace in heaven
and glory in the highest heavens!'

39Some Pharisees in the crowd said to him, 'Master, check your disciples,' 40but he answered, 'I tell you, if these keep silence the stones will cry out.'

The Palm Sunday procession is a living lesson in liturgy. By inviting us to imitate the actions of Jesus entering Jerusalem and the crowd welcoming him, the church wants us to experience that the story is still being lived today. Whenever people of faith decide to confront evil at its source, and do so with inner freedom, remaining faithful to their values, Jesus is once more entering Jerusalem.

We have the same experience by meditating on the gospel texts and recognising ourselves in them.

Each of the gospels tells the story of Jesus' entry into Jerusalem in a distinctive way. In St Luke's account, which we read this year, there is first of all the very significant verse 28, which describes Jesus 'going on ahead of his disciples'.

The events described in verses 29 to 34 are found in all the synoptic accounts, a sign that the early church found them highly symbolical. Some take the story as evidence of Jesus' supernatural powers, but it could merely be evidence of his self-confidence as he faces his great moment of truth, a mark of true leadership.

In St Luke's account, it is the disciples themselves, entering alongside Jesus, who are moved to excitement at this moment.

A small detail, but clearly significant for St Luke: the disciples 'helped Jesus on to the colt'.

The people do not wave palm branches in St Luke's account, but their gesture of spreading their cloaks in the road before Jesus is both a sign of their wild excitement and their welcoming him as a king.

The cry of the people in verse 38 echoes the song of the angels at the birth of Jesus (Lk 2:14).

The brief dialogue in verses 39-40 can be interpreted in different ways. The Pharisees in question may have been followers of Jesus who were afraid of confrontation and wanted to protect Jesus. Or they may have represented the first assault of the opposition to Jesus. In either case his answer expresses his inner freedom very dramatically.

* * *

Lord, there comes a time in the lives of all of us
when we, like Jesus,
must enter into a radical confrontation:
    - those in authority have been abusing their power;
    - we finally recognise that we need help to overcome an addiction;
    - some members of our community have betrayed the cause and must be excluded;
    - we need to give up our comfortable situation and move into something new.
At these moments, give us – and especially those of us
whom you have called to be leaders in our communities –
a share in the inner freedom of Jesus,
so that like him we can go on ahead of the rest,
as we go up to our Jerusalem.

Help us, like Jesus, to make our arrangements
confident that they will come to pass,
and to allow ourselves to be put in a position of authority.
Help us to be so confident of our cause
that if someone told us to check our followers
we would know that if they kept silence,
the stones would cry out.

Lord, we thank you for glorious moments of grace
  - we found a friend whom we felt we could trust perfectly;
  - we enjoyed intimacy with our spouse;
  - one of our children did us proud;
  - a new social movement arose in our country.
We were like the disciples when Jesus approached
the downward slope of the Mount of Olives:
we joyfully began to praise you at the top of our voices
for the miracle which we had seen.
We cried out,
'Blessings on the king who comes in the name of the Lord!'
We glorified you in the highest heavens.

Lord, it is strange how when the moment of grace comes,
everything seems to fall into place very naturally.
If we need something,
we find as the disciples did on the first Palm Sunday,
that all we need say is, 'The Master needs it,'
and immediately all obstacles are removed.

Lord, we pray that as a church
we may not betray our young people.
Often we lack the courage of our convictions,
are too anxious to please them, and do not go ahead of them.
But when young people today meet leaders
who challenge them, they joyfully praise God,
they are ready to spread their cloaks in the road before them,
and welcome them as kings who come in the name of the Lord.

'The important events of history are the thousands of humble actions that heal and reconcile.' Cardinal Arms of Sao Paulo in Brazil, 1994

Lord, we thank you for the many humble people
who enter Jerusalem in peace.
As we think of them, we praise you at the top of our voices
and cry out, 'Peace in heaven and glory in the highest heavens.'

Easter Vigil

Gospel reading: Luke 24:1-12

¹On the first day of the week, at the first sign of dawn, they went to the tomb with the spices they had prepared. ²They found that the stone had been rolled away from the tomb, ³but on entering discovered that the body of the Lord Jesus was not there. ⁴As they stood there not knowing what to think, two men in brilliant clothes suddenly appeared at their side. ⁵Terrified, the women lowered their eyes. But the two men said to them, 'Why look among the dead for someone who is alive? ⁶He is not here; he has risen. Remember what he told you when he was still in Galilee: ⁷that the Son of Man had to be handed over into the power of sinful men and be crucified, and rise again on the third day.' ⁸And they remembered his words.

⁹When the women returned from the tomb they told all this to the Eleven and to all the others. ¹⁰The women were Mary of Magdala, Joanna, and Mary the mother of James. The other women with them also told the apostles, ¹¹but this story of theirs seemed pure nonsense, and they did not believe them. ¹²Peter, however, went running to the tomb. He bent down and saw the binding cloths but nothing else; he then went back home, amazed at what had happened.

The resurrection of Jesus, which we celebrate on this night, is the universal story of God's grace triumphing over evil. Meditating on the biblical texts ahead of the liturgical celebration will help us enter personally into the mystery.

Each of the four gospels tells its own story of how the women discovered that Jesus was risen from the dead. Our meditation must always be based on the text we have before us. Being conscious of what is proper to the author often helps us to read the passage as if for the first time.

St Luke's account, which we read this year, has its own sequence of events. He says that the women discovered first that the body of Jesus was not there; as they were standing there, the angels (two, not one as in Matthew and Mark) announced to them the good news of the resurrection.

Only St Luke includes the words of the angel which express very dramatically the mystery of the resurrection as it is always experienced, 'Why look among the dead for someone who is alive?'

St Luke generally gives more importance to the role of women than the other evangelists. It is significant, then, that in his account the women are not told by the angels to bring the good news to the eleven; they do so of their own accord.

In verses 11 and 12 he highlights the incredulity of the eleven, with a hint that this was 'an old wives' tale'. As always in St Luke, the lowly are raised up while the mighty are cast down from their thrones (1:52).

* * *

'Two men looked out through prison bars; one saw mud, the other stars.' Traditional saying

Lord, we thank you for faithful women,
spouses, mothers, members of our church communities.
When the rest of us give up on others
    - a wayward child,
    - a parish group that has lost its way,
    - a political movement dogged by corruption,
    - a relationship that is going nowhere,
they continue to hope.
What we call the end they see as the first day of a new time,
what we call night they recognise as the first sign of dawn.
Because they are at the tomb with spices they had prepared,
they are the first to discover that the stone has been rolled away
from the tomb and the body is not there;
while we continue to look among the dead
for someone who is alive,
they receive the good news that he is not there
and has risen to new life.

Lord, we thank you for resurrection moments
    - we had given up hope that we would ever be reconciled
with a friend, when all of a sudden we were relating as before;
    - one morning a loved one gave up drink or drugs;
    - a dying friend who had long refused to see a priest asked to do so;
    - opposite sides in a dispute started to negotiate.

We remember how when we understood that the large stone,
which was blocking new life, was now rolled away,
we were like the women at the tomb of Jesus,
we stood there not knowing what to think.
It was all so unexpected that we dared not raise our eyes
in case it was not true.
Only gradually we understood
that we were looking among the dead
for someone who was alive.
We remembered the words we had been told many years before,
that sooner or later we all have to be handed over
into the power of evil,
to be crucified and rise again on the third day.
Thank you, Lord.

*'When we love the other, we obtain from God the key to understanding
who he is and who we are.'* Thomas Merton
Lord, faithful love,
the kind that brings people to a tomb with spices
on the first day of the week and at the first sign of dawn,
is the only power that can roll away the great stone
blocking crucified ones from rising to new life.

*'Lord, look through my eyes, speak through my lips. May my poor
human presence be a reminder, however weak, of your divine presence.'*
Dom Helder Camara
Lord, we pray that in spite of our sins,
our church communities may be signs of hope for society;
that like the two angels in brilliant clothes
who appeared to the women at the tomb of Jesus,
we may announce to those who mourn that,
though it may seem that love has been handed over
into the power of hatred and violence
and securely locked away
with a great stone blocking the way out,
it is not among the dead, but still alive in the world.

Lord, forgive us that we have become so accustomed to evil
– in ourselves, in other people, and in society –
that we have become cynical.
When people speak to us about resurrection and new life
Their story seems to us pure nonsense
and we do not believe them.
Even when, like Peter, we go running to the tomb
and see the cloths that once kept men in bondage
now left lying on the ground,
we merely go back home amazed at what happened
and still do not believe.

'The seed does not see the flower.' Chinese proverb
Lord, we always like to know what the future holds for us.
At this Easter time we think of people of faith
whom we have known
– elderly people in our communities, parents and grandparents,
teachers, founders of a movement we now belong to.
As they walked the roads
of whatever peaceful Galilee they lived in,
they knew a day would come when they would be handed over
into the power of sinful men, perhaps even to be crucified,
but they trusted that with your help
they would rise again on the third day.
Today we remember their words with gratitude.

Easter Sunday

Gospel reading: John 20-1:10

¹*It was very early on the first day of the week, and still dark, when Mary of Magdala came to the tomb. She saw that the stone had been moved away from the tomb* ²*and came running to Simon Peter and the other disciple, the one Jesus loved. 'They have taken the Lord out of the tomb' she said 'and we don't know where they have put him.'* ³*So Peter set out with the other disciple to go to the tomb.*

⁴*They ran together, but the other disciple, running faster than Peter, reached the tomb first;* ⁵*he bent down and saw the linen cloths lying on the ground, but did not go in.* ⁶*Simon Peter who was following now came up, went right into the tomb, saw the linen cloths on the ground,* ⁷*and also the cloth that had been over his head; this was not with the linen cloths but rolled up in a place by itself.*

⁸*Then the other disciple who had reached the tomb first also went in; he saw and he believed.* ⁹*Till this moment they had failed to understand the teaching of scripture, that he must rise from the dead.*

¹⁰*The disciples then went home again.*

John's account of the resurrection is in two stages:
- verses 1-2 are about Mary of Magdala's experience;
- verses 3 to 10 tell us about the experience of the two disciples.

In verses 1 and 2 you might like to focus on the symbolism of it being 'still dark' and yet a 'first day' of a new time. The large stone symbolises all the forces, human and other, that keep God's grace in the bondage of the tomb.

Your experience will help you interpret how Mary responded. Did she run in confusion? Or in fear?

The story of Peter and the disciple whom Jesus loved can be read from various points of view. You can take them together as experiencing the resurrection, focusing on the details, especially the cloths lying on the ground, useless now since Jesus was alive, but also on the fact that until they saw the empty tomb they did not believe the teaching of the scriptures.

St John makes a point of contrasting the two apostles. If you would like to meditate on this aspect of the story, see Peter as

symbol of the church leader, while 'the other disciple' is the one
who, while having no position of authority, is specially loved by
Jesus and, perhaps as a result, is first in faith.

* * *

Lord, we thank you for moments of grace.
We had been in a situation of death
    - a relationship that meant a lot to us seemed dead
    - an addiction held us in its grip
    - our country was locked in civil strife.
Then the day came that would turn out to be
the first of a new era.
We were mourning as usual,
like Mary of Magdala
making a routine visit to the tomb of Jesus,
but saw that the stone had been moved away from the tomb.
Naturally, we looked for some simple explanation,
'they have taken the Lord out of the tomb and we don't know
where they have put him,'
but it wasn't anything like that,
it was what the scriptures teach us,
that your work must always rise again.

'They can kill a bishop, but they cannot kill the church which is the people.' Archbishop Romero, some days before he was martyred
Lord, we thank you for people of faith.
They believe the teaching of the scriptures
that your work may lie in the tomb for some days
but it must rise again.

*'When the underprivileged unite and struggle for justice, is that not a
sign of the presence and action of God in our time?'* Musumi Kanyaro,
Committee of Women in Church and Society, Lutheran World Federation
Lord, as we look around the world today
we see what Peter and the disciple whom Jesus loved
saw as they entered his tomb.
Cloths are lying on the ground
that we can recognise for what they are
– attitudes of passivity that look like fine linen

but in fact kept your chosen ones in the tomb.
Whereas you have once more fulfilled
what you taught us in all the scriptures
and we had not really believed until this moment:
that you will always raise up your chosen ones
when the world imprisons them in a tomb.

Lord, we pray today for those who were baptised last night.
Today they have enthusiasm,
for them you are alive and present;
but there will certainly come a time
when they will experience you absent,
when prayer will be like Mary of Magdala
going in the gloom of early morning to visit the tomb of Jesus.
In fact they will be like people who mourn for a spouse or a child
without even having the comfort of the dead body to look at.
This is the way they will have to pass
because until they have had experiences like this
they will not really believe the teaching of the scriptures
that your grace cannot be overpowered by evil
and that your presence within us
must always, like Jesus, rise again from the tomb.

Lord, we like to feel that we have you within our grasp:
    - that our prayers are always answered;
    - that we are living in a way that is pleasing to you;
    - that the times, gestures and words of our prayers are just
    right.
Teach us that we must be prepared to lose that security
and experience being abandoned, until we live in trust only
and see all those things that we considered important
– like the cloths in the empty tomb of Jesus –
fine linen cloths, but they were keeping him in the tomb.
Now we see them on the ground
and also the cloth that had been over his head
not with the linen cloths but rolled up in a place by itself.

Second Sunday of Easter

Gospel reading: John 20:19-31

^{19}*In the evening of the same day, the first day of the week, the doors were closed in the room where the disciples were, for fear of the Jews. Jesus came and stood among them. He said to them, 'Peace be with you,'* ^{20}*and showed them his hands and his side. The disciples were filled with joy when they saw the Lord,* ^{21}*and he said to them again, 'Peace be with you. As the Father sent me, so am I sending you.'* ^{22}*After saying this he breathed on them and said, 'Receive the Holy Spirit.* ^{23}*For those whose sins you forgive, they are forgiven; for those whose sins you retain, they are retained.'*

^{24}*Thomas, called the Twin, who was one of the Twelve, was not with them when Jesus came.* ^{25}*When the disciples said, 'We have seen the Lord,' he answered, 'Unless I see the holes that the nails made in his hands and can put my finger into the holes they made, and unless I can put my hand into his side, I refuse to believe.'* ^{26}*Eight days later the disciples were in the house again and Thomas was with them. The doors were closed, but Jesus came in and stood among them. 'Peace be with you' he said.* ^{27}*Then he spoke to Thomas, 'Put your finger here; look, here are my hands. Give me your hand; put it into my side. Doubt no longer but believe.'* ^{28}*Thomas replied, 'My Lord and my God!'* ^{29}*Jesus said to him: 'You believe because you can see me. Happy are those who have not seen and yet believe.'*

^{30}*There were many other signs that Jesus worked and the disciples saw, but they are not recorded in this book.* ^{31}*These are recorded so that you may believe that Jesus is the Christ, the Son of God, and believing this you may have life through his name.*

Today's gospel reading, like all of St John's gospel, is an inter-weaving of several themes. It is not possible to follow up all the themes together; we must focus on one at a time, going deeply into it and allowing it to reveal some deep truth about Jesus, about ourselves and about life.

Here I invite you to focus on the apostle Thomas; this is in ac-cord with the Catholic Church's liturgical tradition for the Second Sunday of Easter. Therefore, although the reading in-cludes two of Jesus' resurrection appearances – both of them deeply moving – we stay with the second, the dialogue between Jesus and Thomas, and let the earlier appearance provide the context.

We are free to identify either with Thomas or with Jesus, but not with both at the same time.

We need to be clear on how we understand Thomas. The popular interpretation puts him in a bad light, as 'doubting Thomas'. This however is not the movement of the text, which culminates in Thomas' admirable act of faith, the most explicit in the New Testament – 'My Lord and my God!'

We are more in accord with the spirit of the text, therefore, when we look at Thomas as a model of faith. He was right to insist that before he could believe in Jesus' resurrection he must see the holes the nails made in his hands, put his finger into the holes and his hand into the great wound made by the centurion's lance.

Thomas teaches us the important lesson that we must not separate the resurrection from the cross, since we are called to be followers of Jesus. He also teaches us the truth of the church and of our individual spiritual growth. We cannot live the life of grace, the 'risen life', authentically unless we bear in our bodies the wounds of the cross. This means being conscious that we develop the capacity to love and to be loved only by dying to ourselves.

Our wounds are also a constant reminder of our frailty, and that it is God's grace that raises us up to new life.

St Paul's epistles show that the first Christians needed the corrective of Thomas' faith. They tended to relate with the risen Jesus without reference to his crucifixion. They forgot that they were called to be 'followers of Jesus crucified', choosing to die with him so that they could rise with him (see especially 1 Cor 1).

We Christians fall into the same error today when our lives and our teachings proclaim an abstract 'disembodied' Jesus, dispenser of graces and teacher of morality – we forget the historical person who was put to death for proclaiming the kingdom of God.

Thomas professes the true faith of the church. We too must insist that the Jesus we follow is the true Jesus, the one whose risen body bears the wounds of Calvary.

Jesus is the model leader and spiritual guide. He is pleased to give Thomas the assurance he is looking for, and then challenges him to look forward to the day when he will believe without seeing – always in the Jesus who passes through death to resurrection.

The blessedness of believing without seeing came from the experience of the early church. Jesus is not moralising, but inviting Thomas – and us – to celebrate great people of faith, in our local communities and worldwide, who take up their cross with confidence in the resurrection.

As always in our meditation we must not limit ourselves to personal relationships. We celebrate the resurrection faith lived by communities, nations and cultures.

* * *

'You who remain ever faithful even when we are unfaithful, forgive our sins and grant that we may bear true witness to you before all men and women.' Pope John Paul II, Service of Forgiveness, March 2000

Lord, we thank you for the moments of grace
of this Lenten season,
when – as individuals and as a church community –
we walked in the footsteps of Jesus
by passing from death to new life.
We thank you in particular for the great day
when our church publicly asked forgiveness
from other religions and cultures.
We thank you for Pope John Paul
who, like Jesus with St Thomas,
invited us to see the holes that the nails of arrogance
and self-righteousness had made in the body of Christ,
and to put our fingers into the holes,
to put our hands into the huge wound
which the lust for power has made in his side,
so that we could recognise how,
just as you raised Jesus from the dead,
you do not allow his Body, the church, to remain in the tomb,
but always raise her up to new life.

Lord, we thank you for the times
when reconciliation emerged triumphantly
from the tomb of conflict:
  - the spirit of dialogue between our church and Jews,
  Muslims, Hindus, and African traditional religions;
  - the European Union created by former enemies;
  - the Good Friday agreement in Northern Ireland;
  - the peace process in the Middle East.
Lord, we thank you for the experience of the military in Iraq.
We pray that they will hear your voice calling on them all
to remember those who have been hurt,
who still have holes that the nails made in their hands
and can put their finger into the holes they made,
and unless they can put their hands into their side,
they will refuse to believe.
Do not let us forget the terrible legacy of hatred and resentment
which had to be overcome;
invite us to put our fingers into the holes made by nails,
our hands into the great wounds made by lances,
so that we can recognise with awe and wonder
the spark of your divine life that is within us all.
Remind us too of those who worked for peace
during the long years of conflict
when it seemed that they were working in vain.
How blessed were they who did not see
and yet continued to believe in your power
to bring new life into the world.

'Whoever sees anything of God, sees nothing of God.' Meister Eckhart
Lord, lead us to the blessedness of not seeing, and believing.

'Go for broke, always try to do too much, dispense with safety nets, aim
for the stars.' Salman Rushdie
Lord, we thank you for friends, leaders and spiritual guides
who challenge us as Jesus challenged Thomas.
When we commit ourselves to a cause
because we have tested its reality,
they invite us to experience the blessedness
of believing without seeing.

'Beware of the seduction of leaving the poor to think about them.'
Jean Vanier
Lord, forgive us that we want to help those in need
without sharing their pain,
we look for their resurrection
but do not want to see their wounds:
> - young people have been deeply hurt and we serve them
> with pious exhortations;
> - we become impatient with those who continue to mourn
> the death of a spouse or a child;
> - we think we can restore a broken relationship by merely
> saying we are sorry;
> - we propose reconciliation between warring factions with-
> out acknowledging past wrongs;
> - we pray for peace in the world and do not agonise over its
> terrible injustices.

We thank you for people like Thomas
who will not let us get away with easy solutions;
they insist that we must see
the holes that nails have made in the hands of victims,
put our fingers into the holes
and our hands into wounds that lances have made in their sides,
and only then believe that they have within them
the capacity to rise to new life.

*'We admitted to God, to ourselves, and to another human being, the
exact nature of our wrongs.'* Step 5 in the 12 Step Method of Alcoholics
Anonymous
Lord, when we are converted from an addiction
to alcohol, drugs, power or sex,
we are so anxious to make a new start
that we try to forget the hurt
which was at the root of our problem
> - the loneliness of our childhood
> - the sense of racial inferiority
> - our disability
> - the fear of failure.

We thank you for sending us friends who insist
that we must face the reality of the past.

We pray that, like Jesus welcoming Thomas,
we will invite them to put their fingers into the holes
the nails have made
and their hands into our sides,
so that they can walk with us in our new life.

Third Sunday of Easter

Gospel reading: John 21:1-19

¹*Jesus showed himself again to the disciples. It was by the Sea of Tiberias, and it happened like this:* ²*Simon Peter, Thomas called the Twin, Nathaniel from Cana in Galilee, the sons of Zebedee and two more of his disciples were together.* ³*Simon Peter said, 'I'm going fishing.' They replied, 'We'll come with you.' They went out and got into the boat but caught nothing that night.* ⁴*It was light by now and there stood Jesus on the shore, though the disciples did not realise that it was Jesus.* ⁵*Jesus called out, 'Have you caught anything, friends?' And when they answered, 'No',* ⁶*he said, 'Throw the net out to starboard and you'll find something.' So they dropped the net, and there were so many fish that they could not haul it in.*

⁷*The disciple Jesus loved said to Peter, 'It is the Lord.' At these words 'It is the Lord', Simon Peter, who had practically nothing on, wrapped his cloak round him and jumped into the water.* ⁸*The other disciples came on in the boat, towing the net and the fish; they were only about a hundred yards from land.* ⁹*As soon as they came ashore they saw that there was some bread there, and a charcoal fire with fish cooking on it.* ¹⁰*Jesus said, 'Bring some of the fish you have just caught.'* ¹¹*Simon Peter went aboard and dragged the net to the shore, full of big fish, one hundred and fifty-three of them; and in spite of there being so many the net was not broken.* ¹²*Jesus said to them, 'Come and have breakfast.' None of the disciples was bold enough to ask, 'Who are you?'; they knew quite well it was the Lord.* ¹³*Jesus then stepped forward, took the bread and gave it to them, and the same with the fish.* ¹⁴*This was the third time that Jesus showed himself to the disciples after rising from the dead.*

¹⁵*After the meal Jesus said to Simon Peter, 'Simon son of John, do you love me more than these others do?' He answered, 'Yes, Lord, you know I love you.' Jesus said to him, 'Feed my lambs.'* ¹⁶*A second time he said to him, 'Simon son of John, do you love me?' He replied, 'Yes, Lord, you know I love you.' Jesus said to him, 'Look after my sheep.'* ¹⁷*Then he said to him a third time, 'Simon son of John, do you love me?' Peter was upset that he asked him the third time, 'Do you love me?' and said, 'Lord, you know everything; you know I love you.' Jesus said to him, 'Feed my sheep.* ¹⁸*I tell you most solemnly, when you were young you*

*put on your own belt and walked where you liked; but when you grow
old you will stretch out your hands, and somebody else will put a belt
round you and take you where you would rather not go.' [19]In these
words he indicated the kind of death by which Peter would give glory to
God. After that he said, 'Follow me.'*

During Easter the Sunday and weekday gospel readings are
taken from St John's gospel; this is the time of year when the
church invites us to meditate on this gospel. St John is always
very deep; traditionally his is known as 'the spiritual gospel';
these weeks should therefore be a time for us to deepen our
meditations.

The passage for this coming Sunday is rather long and is a
collection of different incidents. You will have to decide which
of these to concentrate on. To get the full force of the passage,
remember that these incidents are told as if Jesus had not yet appeared to the disciples after his resurrection.

Verses 1 to 8 tell us the story of the miraculous catch. It is
symbolic of what happens to us when we have experienced
death and then experience resurrection. You might, however,
prefer to concentrate on the role of Jesus.

Verses 9 to 14 are another story of a resurrection experience;
here the stress is on Jesus welcoming the disciples.

In verses 15 to 17 Jesus welcomes Peter back into friendship
with him. The connection between loving Jesus and feeding his
sheep is significant.

Verse 18 is a word on the destiny of Peter which is the destiny of all who live long in the service of a cause.

There is a story of Peter running through the passage which
you might like to look at, identifying with this most likeable
character; you will find this story in verses 2, 7, and 11.

* * *

Lord, we remember with gratitude our resurrection experiences:
    * our marriage, or a deep friendship, had collapsed,
    * a movement we believed in had broken up because of inter-
    nal feuding,
    * we had unexpectedly lost our job.
We went about our daily tasks, but without enthusiasm,

just going through the motions,
like Simon Peter saying 'I am going fishing'
and the others answering 'We'll come with you.'
Nothing worked; it was a case of going out in the boat
and catching nothing all night.
Gradually, however, as the weeks went by,
a little light appeared,
an inner voice told us that it was time to try again.
And suddenly things began to come right,
there were so many fish we could not haul them in.
We know now that the inner voice was your presence within us,
a presence that never fails us
even though we don't always recognise it at first,
like the disciples not realising
that it was Jesus standing on the shore.

Lord, send us leaders like Jesus who,
when people are struggling,
do not harangue them,
but stand alongside and offer advice so discreetly
that the people do not know they are there,
but it turns out to be just the right word,
and the people once more discover their creativity.

Lord, we thank you for people who have forgiven us,
not a mean or calculating forgiveness,
not harping on the ways in which we wronged them,
but forgiving with the forgiveness of Jesus,
so that it was like coming back from a hard night's work
and seeing some bread there
and a charcoal fire with fish cooking on it
and the very person we had hurt saying
'Come and have breakfast,'
and we not having to ask any questions
because we knew that everything was forgiven.

'The best dreams of humanity are born in the night.' Elie Weisel
Lord, we thank you for the great achievements
that grew out of times of suffering:
    - the courage of the Jews during the Holocaust,
    - the creativity of slaves in the last century,
    - the non-violence of those who fought for civil rights in the
    sixties.
They were the huge catch of fish the disciples made,
so many that they could not haul them in.

Lord, we pray for those who train minister in your church.
Teach them to call these future ministers to them
as Jesus called Simon Peter, asking them, do they love Jesus?
And not to be satisfied with asking them once,
but to ask three times, even if this upsets them,
because it is only if they have a personal relationship with Jesus
that they are fit to pasture his sheep.

Lord, we pray for those who are getting married at this time.
Remind them that their commitment is for ever,
and that at one time in a relationship
we are strong and walk where we like,
but another time comes
when we have to stretch out our hands for help
and let the other person take charge of us,
even taking us where we would rather not go.

Fourth Sunday of Easter

Gospel reading: John 10:27-30

27Jesus said, 'The sheep that belong to me listen to my voice; I know them and they follow me. 28I give them eternal life; they will never be lost and no one will ever steal them from me. 29The Father who gave them to me is greater than anyone, and no one can steal from the Father. 30The Father and I are one.

On the fourth Sunday of Easter the gospel reading is always taken from chapter 10 of St John's gospel – the chapter in which is developed the theme of the Good Shepherd. A different extract from this chapter is read each year of the three-year cycle; we read the shortest one of the three in Year C.

The Good Shepherd passages tell us about Jesus, but also about all who have been given authority over others – parents, teachers, community leaders or spiritual guides. As we meditate on these passages, we therefore think with gratitude of good shepherds we have known. Your meditation could also be an examination of conscience on how you exercise authority.

The passage develops three themes:

- in verse 27 the sheep obey not because of any external compulsion, but because they experience that they belong to the shepherd and are known by him;

- in verse 28 the shepherd is perfectly secure in the loyalty of the sheep. Good shepherds don't have to wonder, 'Am I loved?' or 'Are the sheep loyal to me?' They can therefore set about the work of leadership in freedom. Secure in their role, they can be creative, try new things, pose new challenges.

- In verses 29 and 30 we see that the security of good shepherds is rooted in their union with God.

It is traditional on this Sunday to remember ministers in the church, so you might orient your meditation specially in that direction. Make sure you include in your meditation the whole range of 'ministers' in a modern church community – parish council members, lectors, ministers of the Eucharist, spiritual guides, choir leaders, finance committee members, directors of organisations such as St Vincent de Paul, prayer groups, etc.

'If you have come to help me you are wasting your time. But if you have come because your liberation is bound up with mine, then let us work together.' An Australian Aboriginal

Lord, we pray for those who work in community development.
They often find that they cannot motivate people
or get them to change their ways,
and they think that what people need
is to take courses or develop new skills.
But Jesus taught us the secret of being shepherds:
if people don't feel that they belong to us
they will not hear our voice,
and unless they get the feeling that we know them
they won't follow us.

Lord we thank you for deep relationships:
    - a spouse, an intimate friend, a leader to whom we entrusted
    ourselves,
    - a priest who ministered to us.
We remember how the very first time we met
we knew that we belonged to them, and recognised their voice;
we felt that they knew us through and through,
and spontaneously we followed them.

Lord, there are people in our country
who are always talked down to
because they are considered uneducated or unintelligent.
We pray that at least in our church communities
they may know that they belong,
that leaders know them and accept them for who they are.

Lord, one of the frustrating things about being a teacher
is that we wonder if we are getting through to our students.
But every once in a while
you send us someone who is your special gift to us,
someone we know instinctively belongs to us and follows us;
we know they might stray for a while,
but they will never be lost or stolen from us.

Lord, when people we love leave us we become jealous:
  - our followers turn to another leader;
  - a favourite child starts to show a preference for the other
  parent;
  - a friend gets close to someone else.
Even as a church we are jealous
when members join another church.
Lord, at the root of all jealousy is insecurity.
If we were more like Jesus
we would accept those you give us with trust,
knowing that if they are really your gift to us
then no one can steal them from us
because you are greater than anyone
and no one can steal from you.

'Bind us with cords that cannot be broken.' Popular hymn
Lord, we thank you for moments of deep prayer
when we feel perfectly secure,
so that we don't need to ask for anything,
to beg for forgiveness or to make promises.
We know that in Jesus we and you are one
and we are one with all creation,
because everything is your gift and you are greater than anyone,
and no power in heaven or on earth can steal from you.

Fifth Sunday of Easter

Gospel reading: John 13:31-35

[31]*When Judas had gone from the upper room, Jesus said: 'Now has the Son of Man been glorified, and in him God has been glorified.* [32]*If God has been glorified in him, God will in turn glorify him in himself, and will glorify him very soon.* [33]*My little children, I shall not be with you much longer. You will look for me, and, as I told the Jews, where I am going, you cannot come.* [34]*I give you a new commandment: love one another; just as I have loved you, you also must love one another.* [35]*By this love you have for one another, everyone will know that you are my disciples.'*

It is traditional in the church that on the 5th and 6th Sundays of the Easter season, the gospel readings are taken from the long discourse which St John tells us Jesus had with the apostles at the Last Supper, and which is recounted from chapter 13:31 to the end of chapter 17. This is very deep teaching, so you must make a special effort to experience that it is also down-to-earth, and helps you to understand your own life.

This year's first extract is the beginning of the discourse. It is in clearly distinct sections:

Verses 31 and 32 are the response of Jesus to the departure of Judas. You may have difficulty interpreting the word 'glorify' which occurs several times. It is a biblical term indicating the victory of God's power. It is significant that 'hallowed' in the first petition of the Our Father means the same thing.

In verse 33, Jesus says clearly that he is at a point in his life when he must make his journey alone. The saying is repeated and clarified in verse 36, which is not included in this passage, but which you may want to look up in a Bible.

In verses 34 and 35 the commandment of love – which is the dominant theme of the last discourse – is enunciated for the first time. Read the verses carefully, letting them touch you as if you were reading them for the first time.

* * *

'The tyrant dies and his rule ends. The martyr dies and his rule begins.'
Kirkegaard
Lord, we thank you for the great martyrs of our time,
Gandhi, Martin Luther King, Archbishop Romero.
Those who put them to death have long been forgotten,
gone like Judas into the night,
but they have been glorified
and you have been glorified in them.

Lord, there was a time when we struggled
with some sin for several years,
lust, jealousy, racial prejudice, the inability to forgive.
Then one day we knew that this Judas had gone and left us,
that we had been victorious
or rather that you had been victorious in us,
and like Jesus we knew that even if we face a great crisis,
you will be with us and soon bring us to safety with you.

Lord, forgive us that as a church community
we make compromises
in order to please powerful people,
fearing that otherwise they may harm us.
Teach us that sooner or later Judas goes away
and if our trust has been in our fidelity to your teaching,
you will be glorified in us and you will glorify us in yourself.

Lord, all of us who have charge of young people,
as parents, teachers, youth leaders or spiritual guides,
help us not to be possessive as Peter was with Jesus,
wondering why we cannot accompany them in all their crises,
and looking for them even though they tell us clearly
that where they are going we cannot come.

Lord, there comes a time in life for each of us, as it did for Jesus,
when we have to make a decision alone:
    - to marry;
    - to enter religious life or the seminary;
    - to run for public office;
    - to accept terminal illness.

Often before, we have had to distance ourselves
from those who did not love us.
Now we say to those dearest to us
that where we are going they cannot come.

Lord, we thank you for the time
that we experienced selfless love for someone,
for one of our parents, a friend, a leader in our community.
At that moment it was as if we had understood love
for the first time;
we had received a new commandment to love others
as we had been loved.

Lord, there is a history of love in the world,
so that when we see people
who are able to reach out to one another,
we know that they have experienced love themselves.

'Non-violence is the greatest and most active force in the world.'
Gandhi
Lord, when people love unconditionally, as Jesus did,
everyone knows that your disciples are at work in the world.

Sixth Sunday of Easter

Gospel reading: John 14:23-29

23Jesus said to his disciples, 'If anyone loves me he will keep my word, and my Father will love him, and we shall come to him and make our home in him. 24Those who do not love me do not keep my words. And my word is not my own; it is the word of the one who sent me. 25I have said these things to you while still with you; 26but the Advocate, the Holy Spirit, whom the Father will send in my name, will teach you everything and remind you of all I have said to you.

27Peace I bequeath to you, my own peace I give you, a peace the world cannot give, this is my gift to you. Do not let your hearts be troubled or afraid. 28You hear me say: I am going away, and shall return. If you loved me you would have been glad to know that I am going to the Father, for the Father is greater than I. 29I have told you this now before it happens, so that when it does happen you may believe.'

In this second extract from the last discourse of Jesus we see various aspects of the spiritual life being brought out. The aspects are interconnected, but you can look at them separately if you like.

To understand the full force of verses 23 and 24 you must go to the previous verse, which is not included in this Sunday's reading, where one of the apostles asks Jesus why he will not show himself to the whole world. Jesus' response is to explain that following him involves an inner relationship which cannot be bypassed.

The second half of verse 24, and verses 25 and 26, show us Jesus facing the fact that much of his teaching was unfinished, and still more was misunderstood.

In verse 27 Jesus speaks of how he shares his inner peace with his followers.

In verse 28 he expresses how he is experiencing his imminent death.

In verse 29 he returns to the theme of the existing relationship between the disciples and himself, and contrasts this with how they will experience him after his death and resurrection.

* * *

Lord, many people in our country feel alienated,
they would like to be different from who they are,
to have lived at a different time,
or belonged to a different culture.
We pray that they may come to love someone like Jesus
who will assure them that their stories,
far from being drab or uninteresting, are sacred stories,
and that they need not feel ashamed of who they are
because you, the great Lord and God,
you feel at home with them.

Lord, the apostles often felt frustrated with Jesus;
they could not understand why he spent so much time
with them alone.
They wanted him to hurry and let the whole world know
what he was teaching them.
At one time, we too thought that the message of Jesus
could be packaged
into a few brief commandments
and marketed by radio and television.
Now we know from our experience that becoming his followers
is a personal journey that each one of us
must make for ourselves.
We get a feel for the man Jesus and gradually
we learn to love his words
so that they sink into our consciousness,
until one day we know that you have come into our lives
and whatever happens you will never leave us again.

Lord, we could know all the teachings of Jesus by heart,
but if we don't have a personal relationship with him
we will not keep them.

Lord, when church leaders or State leaders
become cruel or violent
it is because they have come to think that they are indispensable
and have forgotten that they are only your instruments.
Teach them to be like Jesus,
aware that their word is not theirs

but the word of the one who sent them;
that they are here on earth for a short while
saying what they have to say, and they will soon move on.
But that will not be the end of your work,
because you will send the Holy Spirit, the Advocate,
and all the things they have taught he will teach again,
and he will remind people
of whatever they have forgotten or not understood.

'If you desire peace, prepare for war.' Roman proverb
Lord, the great powers can never bring peace to the world
because they want to impose it by force,
whereas, as Jesus taught, we cannot impose peace,
we can only share the peace that we have ourselves
as a gift that others are free to take or leave.

Lord, people have taught us facts and skills,
but there have been a few special people
who have been like Jesus for us
in that they shared with us how they coped with life,
and their courage, their perseverance
is like a precious inheritance
which we can build on in our own lives.

Lord, we thank you for the faith
that enables us to let our loved ones go,
so that we can take leave of them
saying to ourselves, in the midst of our sorrow,
that since we love them
we are glad to know that they are going to you,
their Father in heaven.

Lord, we become attached to the things
which bring us close to you:
    - our devotions and pilgrimages;
    - the way liturgy is celebrated in our parish;
    - our method of prayer.
When we have to give them up
we become anxious and even angry.

But we have learned from experience
that we must not let our hearts be troubled or afraid
because you are greater
than any manifestation of your presence,
and just as Jesus went away from his disciples and returned
so you will always show yourself to us in a new way.

Lord, we thank you for our parents.
Like Jesus with his disciples
they told us things before they happened
and now that they have happened we can believe.

Feast of the Ascension

Gospel reading: Luke 24:46-53

46*Jesus said to his disciples: 'You see how it is written that the Christ would suffer and on the third day rise from the dead, 47and that, in his name, repentance for the forgiveness of sins would be preached to all the nations, beginning from Jerusalem. 48You are witnesses to this. 49And now I am sending down to you what the Father has promised. Stay in the city, then, until you are clothed with the power from on high.'*

50*Then he took them out as far as the outskirts of Bethany, and lifting up his hands he blessed them. 51Now as he blessed them, he withdrew from them and was carried up to heaven. 52They worshipped him and then went back to Jerusalem full of joy; 53and they were continually in the Temple praising God.*

The Ascension of Jesus was an essential stage in his relationship with this followers. He had walked with them in their moments of strength and of weakness, and now he was leaving them.

It is, of course, significant that this moment occurred immediately after his apparent defeat and after they had betrayed him.

By meditating on the story, we discover similar moments in our own relationship with God, with a cause, or with people who have touched our lives.

St Luke tells us the story in three sections:

- Verses 47 and 48 are the conclusion of a teaching by which Jesus 'opened the minds of the apostles to understand the scriptures.' You can interpret 'the scriptures' as referring to all traditional wisdom.

- Verse 49 stands by itself as a dramatic call to wait patiently until the moment of grace.

- Verses 50 to 53 are St Luke's account of the ascension; every word is symbolical.

Discover through your meditation the paradox of the apostles 'returning to Jerusalem full of joy' after such a sorrowful parting.

Lord, we remember a time when we had given ourselves
to a cause and became disillusioned:
> - a trusted companion let us down,
> - the political party we had joined was rejected at the polls,
> - we turned away from an addiction but fell back into it,
> - our church community closed down a movement we had started.

Then something happened to make us realise that the movement was still alive:
> - a new leader took charge,
> - old companions returned and new ones joined us,
> - in a moment of prayer we felt a new heart had been put into us.

It was as if Jesus had appeared to us and said,
'So you see how it is written that an Anointed One must suffer,
and only on the third day rise from the dead.'

'We have closed the book on apartheid.' F. W. De Klerk on television, 18 March 1992. *'Not yet, mister.'* Response of an evangelical pastor
Lord, we pray for the people of South Africa,
and all those who are starting on the path of conversion.
Let them not forget how it is written
that the Christ would suffer
and on the third day rise from the dead.

Lord, we would always prefer to preach the name of Jesus from a position of strength
> - we have turned away from sin;
> - we have completed a course of study and now understand the message;
> - many people admire us.

Send Jesus to remind us
that if we want repentance for the forgiveness of sins
to be preached to all the nations,
we must begin from Jerusalem
where we betrayed our cause and were welcomed back.
Then we will be witnesses to your forgiveness.

'I continue to believe that unarmed truth and unconditional love will have the final word in reality.' Martin Luther King, accepting the Nobel Peace prize

Lord, we pray today for those
who are tired of waiting for your grace
-parents with a child addicted to drugs,
-leaders working for church renewal,
-radical politicians,
-third world people caught in the debt trap.
Though you are delaying,
you are sending down what you promised,
so they must stay in the city
until they are clothed with the power from on high.

'The person of prayer leads the world beyond the dichotomy of life and death and is therefore a witness to life.' Thomas Merton

Lord, we thank you for the great people
you have sent into our lives
- they widened our horizons,
- helped us to see new possibilities,
- showed us the implications of our sins.
Like Jesus with his disciples,
they led us to the outskirts of where we lived,
lifted their hands and blessed us and then withdrew from us,
leaving us to return to our daily lives full of joy.
We were sad, of course, and felt tremendous respect for them,
but their being carried up to heaven did not destroy us.
We went back to Jerusalem full of joy,
and from then on
we were continually in the temple praising you.

Seventh Sunday of Easter

Gospel reading: John 17:20-26

20*Jesus raised his eyes to heaven and said: 'Holy Father, I pray not only for these, but for those also who through their words will believe in me.* 21*May they all be one. Father, may they be one in us as you are in me and I am in you, so that the world may believe it was you who sent me.* 22*I have given them the glory you gave to me, that they may be one as we are one.* 23*With me in them and you in me, may they be so completely one that the world will realise that it was you who sent me and that I have loved them as much as you loved me.*

24*Father, I want those you have given me to be with me where I am, so that they may always see the glory you have given to me because you loved me before the foundation of the world.* 25*Father, Righteous One, the world has not known you, but I have known you, and these have known that you have sent me.* 26*I have made your name known to them and I will continue to make it known, so that the love with which you loved me may be in them, and so that I may be in them.'*

Chapter 17 of John's gospel is a long unbroken prayer, unique in the gospels. Traditionally, it has been called 'the priestly prayer', an appropriate title since the theme of holiness runs right through. It is important to be aware however that what we have here is not prayer in the sense of making petitions, but rather what prayer is at root – a deep experience of communion.

Jesus deals with various themes and we get the opportunity to integrate these teachings into our prayer life. The main theme is a majestic vision of the unity to which the disciples of Jesus and indeed all human beings are called. This unity is seen to sum up the work of Jesus, in direct opposition to fragmentation, which is the work of sin. At the same time, Jesus here is the model for his followers as they face death or any big crisis in their lives.

The passage we have this Sunday brings the prayer to a grand climax. Jesus extends his gaze forward into history, to generations of future believers (verse 20).

He prays as if his earthly life is over and he is already in heaven, at one with the Father. From this experience of unity he looks forward to the unity of believers and their unity with the Father through him.

His perspective remains missionary: the unity of believers will make them credible before 'the world' (verse 23).

He remains down to earth too, conscious that there will be some who are so much 'of the world' that they will not accept the call to unity.

The unity Jesus speaks of here is more than loving; it is a unity of being rooted in the unity of Father, Son and Spirit, a truly mystical vision.

* * *

'What kind of civilisation will prevail in the world's future? It depends on us if it will be the civilisation of love, or the "uncivilisation" of individualism.' Pope John Paul II, February 1994

Lord, all round us we see selfishness at work,
fragmenting families, neighbourhoods,
nations and humanity itself.
We thank you for those who, with Jesus,
belong to another movement
by which we become one humanity, all of us one in you,
you in us, and we in you.

'Everybody want to be King Crab, a lawyer, a executive, a big pappy; nobody want to do no small work and get dey hands dirty.' Miguel Browne, Trinidadian folk poet

Lord, how true it is that the world does not know you.
For the world, glory is
    - kings and queens sitting on thrones with servants at their
    beck and call,
    - military leaders conquering their enemies,
    - scholars showing how much wiser they are than others,
    - sportsmen and women defeating their rivals.
But Jesus has revealed that the glory you gave him
was unity in Trinity, allowing others to be different from us,
and his will is that through us
he should continue to make
this kind of glory present in the world.

'The family draws its proper character as a community from the fundamental communion of the spouses which is prolonged in their children.'
Pope John Paul II, *Letter to Families*, February 1994

Lord, we thank you for parents who love each other
and then love their children
as much as they have loved each other.
The love which they receive from each other
is in their children and they too are in them.

Lord, people turn away from the teachings of Jesus
when they see the various Christian Churches
quarrelling among themselves
and competing with one another for members.
We pray with Jesus that his followers may be so completely one
that the world will realise that it was you who sent him.

Lord, we thank you for moments of oneness
    - walking along the beach at sunset
    - listening to music
    - remaining in silence before you
    - looking at our children at play together
    - celebrating a solemn liturgy.
Quite suddenly, Jesus's prayer is heard, all fragmentation gone,
we are one with those closest to us,
with the whole world, and with ourselves.
The glory you gave to Jesus before the foundation of the world
is in us, and we are with him where he is,
the love with which you loved him
is holding us together in him,
and we are completely one.

'A radical has to be a person of roots, and deep roots, with the freedom and courage, as Jesus had, to go to the source and speak from the centre.' Anglican Bishop John Robinson

Lord, send us leaders like Jesus, who live out of the experience
that you have loved them from the foundation of the world
and desire that love to be in those you have given them to serve.

'While proclaiming the message of God in Jesus Christ, the evangelis-
ing church must always remember that the Holy Spirit, the Spirit of
Christ, is present and active among the hearers of the Good News, even
before the church's missionary action comes into operation.' Vatican
document on Dialogue and Proclamation, July 1991

Lord, we pray that we may preach the gospel of Jesus to others
not arrogantly or possessively,
but humbly, listening as well as speaking,
conscious that your grace is within them
leading them to know you have sent us,
that the same love with which you loved us is in them,
and we too are in them.

Pentecost

Gospel reading: John 14:15-16; 23-26

15Jesus said to his disciples: 'If you love me you will keep my command-ments. 16I shall ask the Father, and he will give you another Advocate to be with you for ever. 23If anyone loves me he will keep my word, and my Father will love him, and we shall come to him and make our home with him. 24Those who do not love me do not keep my words. And my word is not my own; it is the word of the one who sent me. 25I have said these things to you while still with you; 26but the Advocate, the Holy Spirit, whom the Father will send in my name, will teach you every-thing and remind you of all I have said to you.'

Jesus is about to leave his apostles and as he gets ready to do this, he begins to speak to them about something that will hap-pen and will be of tremendous importance for them and for un-derstanding him and where he is coming from.

He tells them of the future coming of the Holy Spirit. He speaks of two things:
- of how close he will be to their own insights
- of what he will teach them, how he will add to what they have already learnt from him.

He makes two radical points which he stresses right through his teaching. Today, after our long distance from the time of Jesus, we look at them with a better understanding of all this implies for us today.

a) The first point is that the Spirit will be true to the teachings of Jesus, those he gave to the apostles and which they must re-tain for ever. These are tremendously important teachings which we must understand today whatever happens. What hap-pens to us does not matter because Jesus was aware of them even from where he stood at the time of his leaving his follow-ers.

b) The second is that the Spirit will often bring out new things – or, rather, things which seem very new to us. In fact, there will be great changes from what the church thought it had learnt directly from Jesus. They will therefore be 'new'.

We can now see more clearly than ever before two important things:

- where the disciples were, what was their ideology, how they looked on their world;
- where Jesus wanted to bring them to and the world in which he wanted them to live.

Let us look at these two aspects of the work of the Spirit as they are revealed in this text.

In verses 15 to 16 Jesus says clearly that the Spirit will be 'old'. The Father knows the Spirit. They will know that whatever he teaches is from the Spirit since the Father has always been 'with him' and he is also 'in him'. It is essential then that those who follow the Spirit always make the link between what Jesus said and what they now believe.

On the other hand, he will come with something that seems new. He will conquer whatever weaknesses people will be able to discover in Jesus' revelations. He will say things which 'the world cannot receive' since it does not know him nor his full revelation.

In verses 23 to 24, the teaching of the Spirit is 'old' in the sense that we shall always come back to Jesus. We will always learn new things from him, from what he revealed to them. Whatever he inspires in us, we will eventually learn to love the Father in him, and Jesus too will make his home with him.

It is 'new' in the sense that what he will say will be what he has learnt from the other two. We who love him will find in his words 'the word of the one who sent him'. He will be revealing what he has learnt from the other members of the Trinity.

In verses 25 to 26, his teaching is 'old' in the sense that his word is not his own but the word of the one who sent him. This is Jesus who 'has said all these things to him from the beginning'. His words are all lasting therefore and will remain valid whatever happens in the future.

His teaching will also be 'new'. 'The Advocate, the Holy Spirit whom the Father will send in my name', he will 'teach you everything and remind you of all I have said to you'. The Spirit will therefore remind the disciples of all Jesus said to them as he faced his passion.

* * *

'If you wish to attain your being in which God created you, in all noble-ness, you must not reform any difficulty, with all the hardiness and prize you must neglect nothing but valiantly seize the best part. I mean the totality of God as your wealth.' Blessed Hadewight of the Holy Beguines

Lord, we pray for the grace to remember the teachings of Jesus.
Help us to recognise his presence among us
and to look forward to them.
We thank you for sending your Holy Spirit
into our church of today.
We thank you that the work of the Spirit is new
and we must learn many things
from what we now see happening in our present world.
It is also old, however, and it must always return us
to the original teaching of Jesus
and of the Father who spoke through him.
We realise today how many wonderful things we can learn
from the newly established importance
of women in the world today,
from all they have done.
We must now re-learn and re-discover
the many things he taught us
and which became lost in the all-male world
in which they grew and developed.
We remember today the great things
    - within our church,
    - in the world as we relate with it apart from the church,
    - in the secular world which makes no reference to the church
    in its findings and discoveries.
We think today of the many things we learn
from those who belong to other Christian religions,
which we had tended to look down on.
We remember with great sadness
    - the distance maintained by the Roman Pontiffs and other
    leaders of our church in the face of the founding of the World
    Council of Churches and other ecumenical work in the world;
    - we remember similar attitudes, maintained by the leaders
    of other churches, when they found that their own insights
    were no longer accepted by our church and so considered
    themselves far from us.

We think today of the many things we have learnt
from those who follow other religions
which we once considered far from ours.
We think of those who follow other religions
tied to the people of the East,
the followers of Confucius, Buddha, the *Bhagavad Gita*
and other Eastern sages.
Help us, Lord, in our time to welcome them among us
and to learn from them.
We remember the great sages of the Muslim faith.
We thank you for what they can now teach us
in our faith and understanding.
We think of those who belong to the great religions of Africa,
and also of North and South America.
We thank you for the wonderful lessons
we have learnt from them
    - their sense of the greatness of God, present in every creature,
    - their sense of the protection of every person on earth,
    - their connection with all who have died.
We remember the very great people
who have been torn away from our fold
for what they have seen wrong.
They now seem to have no religion at all.
We thank you for all that we have learnt from them.

Trinity Sunday

Gospel reading: John 16: 12-15

12Jesus said to his disciples: 'I still have many things to say to you but they would be too much for you now. 13But when the Spirit of truth comes he will lead you to the complete truth, since he will not be speaking as from himself but will say only what he has learnt; and he will tell you of the things to come. 14He will glorify me, since all he tells you will be taken from what is mine. 15Everything the Father has is mine; that is why I said: All he tells you will be taken from what is mine.'

We meet two kinds of feasts in the liturgy. The most important are the mysteries, incidents in the life of Jesus which we enter into, experiencing them as living again in us – we have just completed the cycle of the Easter mysteries.

Now the church invites us to celebrate three of the second kind of feasts – the Trinity, Corpus Christi, and the Sacred Heart of Jesus.

In these feasts we celebrate some aspect of our faith. It is a celebration, therefore, not an academic exercise. Meditating on the gospel texts chosen for each feast helps us enter into it.

It is particularly important to do this for the Trinity, because this doctrine is usually experienced as a mathematical sum to be learnt, rather than good news to be celebrated.

The gospel text for the feast this year will seem forbidding at first. But as with many of the teachings of Jesus recorded in St John's gospel, if you read it imaginatively you will find that it will come alive.

Feel free to take the passage as you will, but it is good to let it speak to you about the Trinity. Jesus is the model of what believing in the Trinity does for us.

It is helpful to situate the passage in its context: it is a moment of separation, Jesus is giving his followers a last teaching before leaving them.

* * *

'Consult not your fears but your hopes and dreams. Think not about your frustrations but about your potential.' Pope John Paul II

Lord, as parents and teachers we tend to become self-important
- we think we have to tell our charges everything they need to know,
- preserve them from making mistakes,
- prepare them for every eventuality.

Help us to be humble like Jesus,
knowing that no matter how much we do for people,
there are always things that we still have to say to them,
but these things would be too much for them
at this point in their lives.
We need not be anxious about that,
because when the time comes,
the Spirit of truth will come
and will lead them to the complete truth.

'Someone who knows his own weakness is greater than someone who sees the angels.' Isaac of Nineveh, Syrian monk of the 7th century

Lord, there are many factions in the church,
each one thinking they have the complete truth.
Help us to be a church modeled on your Holy Trinity,
aware that none of us possesses the complete truth
since that belongs to you alone.
We do not speak as from ourselves,
but only what we have received from you as your gift.
When we understand that,
we can really prepare people for the things to come.

'When the archer shoots for no particular prize, he has all his skills; when he shoots to win, he thinks more of winning than of shooting, and the need to win drains him of power.' Tranxu, Chinese sage

Lord, like Jesus, we need not be anxious for success.
Whatever happens in the future will glorify us
since it will be taken from what is ours.
That may seem a presumptuous thing to say, but it isn't.
We say it because we know that everything you have is ours.

'My son, you are with me always, and all I have is yours.' The father in
the parable of the prodigal son, Luke 15:31
Lord, you treat us like members of your family,
and share everything you have with us.
When we think we must earn goodness by our hard work,
>   - we become jealous of others;
>   - angry that they do not recognise what they owe us;
>   - self-righteous that our words have been proved right.
If, like Jesus, we remember that everything you have is ours,
we rejoice in the gifts of others.

Lord, forgive us that as followers of Jesus,
we think we have a monopoly,
or even a first option, on the truth.
Teach us to welcome truth wherever we find it;
remind us that Jesus was not possessive of the truth;
he knew that everything you have is his,
and so everything the Spirit would tell the world
until the end of time
would be taken from what was his.

Lord, noble ideals are handed on to us
by great people who went before us.
When we strive for those ideals, we glorify them,
since all we do is taken from what is theirs.

*'Nothing that happened in Eastern Europe in these last years would
have been possible without the presence of this Pope.'* Former Soviet
President Mikhail Gorbachev, March 1992
Lord, we thank you for Pope John Paul II
and spiritual people like him.
Guided by the Spirit, they do not speak as from themselves,
but say only what they have learnt,
and so they tell the world of things to come.

The Body and Blood of Christ

¹¹*Jesus made the crowds welcome, and talked to them about the kingdom of God; and he cured those who were in need of healing.* ¹²*It was late afternoon when the Twelve came to him and said, 'Send the people away, and they can go to the villages and farms round about to find lodging and food; for we are in a lonely place here.'* ¹³*He replied, 'Give them something to eat yourselves.' But they said, 'We have no more than five loaves and two fish, unless we are to go ourselves and buy food for all these people.'* ¹⁴*For there were about five thousand men. But he said to his disciples, 'Get them to sit down in parties of about fifty.'* ¹⁵*They did so and made them all sit down.* ¹⁶*Then he took the five loaves and the two fish, raised his eyes to heaven, and said the blessing over them; then he broke them and handed them to his disciples to distribute among the crowd.* ¹⁷*They all ate as much as they wanted, and when the scraps remaining were collected they filled twelve baskets.*

Corpus Christi is an occasion for us to celebrate the sacrament of the Eucharist. It should also be an occasion when we enter into the symbolism of this great sacrament, letting it teach us deep lessons about life, our relationship with God and with one another. Meditation on the readings for the feast will help us to celebrate the feast in both ways.

St Luke's account of the miraculous feeding is very helpful as it is both a teaching on the Eucharist and on Jesus' way of relating with people.

The story is introduced in verse 11 by a brief summary of Jesus' ministry: 'talking about the kingdom' is a powerful expression referring to the goal of his life.

Feel free to enter into the story of the feeding at whatever stage touches you.

Verses 12 to 14a set the stage for the miracle. Note the contrasting responses of Jesus and the twelve.

Verses 14b to 16 describe the feeding. The gestures of Jesus are reminiscent of the Eucharist, but are highly significant in themselves. So, too, verse 17 is symbolical both of the Eucharist and of life.

Lord, we thank you for the Holy Eucharist.
Every Sunday, all over the world,
people sit down in their church communities.
The priest takes the bread and wine,
raises his eyes to heaven and says the blessing over them,
then he breaks the bread and distributes it among the crowd.
We all get as much nourishment as we want,
and when we are finished the remains of the bread
is collected and reverently stored.

Lord, many in our country are being fed
with nourishment that is unworthy of their humanity.
We pray that those of us to whom you have given
the priceless gift of education
may be like Jesus in our society, making the crowds welcome,
talking to them about the glorious kingdom
you have prepared for us,
curing all those who need to be healed.

'The poor must recover their hope.' Pope John Paul II in Haiti, 1982
Lord, we pray that in every country
your church may be the presence of Jesus,
curing the poor of the terrible disease of despair,
speaking to them about the kingdom
you are establishing in the world.

'The world has enough for every man's need, but not enough for every man's greed.' Gandhi
Lord, often today we see pictures of hungry people,
  - mothers with ghostly babies at their breasts,
  - children with swollen bellies,
  - long lines of people outside food stores.
Like the disciples of Jesus, we say,
'Why can't they go to villages and farms round about them
to find lodging and food?'
Now and then the thought comes to us
that we should give them something to eat ourselves,
but we quickly dismiss that as impractical.
We find all kinds of excuses:

    - we are in a lonely place here;
     - we have no more than five loaves and two fish;
     - are we to go ourselves and buy food for all these people?
Lord, your solution is really quite simple:
sit people down in small communities;
take whatever five loaves and two fish you have;
raise your eyes to heaven and say the blessing over them;
break the bread and hand it around
to be distributed among the crowd.
Not only would all eat as much as they want,
but when the remaining scraps are collected,
we will fill many baskets.

Lord, it is an extraordinary thing:
if we complain about the little we have, we never have enough;
but if we take what we have,
raise our eyes to heaven and say the blessing over it,
we have as much as we want,
and even twelve baskets of scraps left over.

'People come to us looking for the bread of compassion and we give
them the stone of advice.' A modern psychologist
Lord, so long as we look on people as objects of our attention,
saying to ourselves that when late afternoon comes
we will send them away to the villages
and farms round about to find lodging and food,
and that we don't have to give them something to eat
from the five loaves and two fish we have,
we will never be true followers of Jesus.
Lord, have mercy.

Second Sunday in Ordinary Time

Gospel reading: John 2:1-11

¹*There was a wedding in Cana in Galilee. The mother of Jesus was there,* ²*and Jesus and his disciples had also been invited.* ³*When they ran out of wine, since the wine provided for the wedding was all finished, the mother of Jesus said to him, 'They have no wine.'* ⁴*Jesus said, 'Woman, why turn to me? My hour has not come yet.'* ⁵*His mother said to the servants, 'Do whatever he tells you.'*

⁶*There were six stone jars standing there, meant for the ablutions that are customary among the Jews; each could hold twenty to thirty gallons.* ⁷*Jesus said to the servants, 'Fill the jars with water,' and they filled them to the brim.* ⁸*'Draw some out now' he told them 'and take it to the steward.'* ⁹*They did this; the steward tasted the water, and it had turned into wine. Having no idea where it came from – only the servants who had drawn the water knew – the steward called the bridegroom* ¹⁰*and said, 'People generally serve the best wine first, and keep the cheaper sort till the guests have had plenty to drink; but you have kept the best wine till now.'*

¹¹*This was the first of the signs given by Jesus; it was given at Cana in Galilee. He let his glory be seen, and his disciples believed in him.*

Sunday in the liturgy is always 'the first day of the week,' so since Ordinary Time starts on the Monday after the Epiphany, this Sunday is called the Second Sunday of Ordinary Time.

We might expect to start immediately with the continuous reading from the synoptic gospel for the year, which characterises Ordinary Time. However, liturgical custom dictates otherwise: on this Sunday each year we meditate on a passage from the first chapters of St John's gospel. It is as if the church is reluctant to say farewell to the Christmas season – or perhaps reluctant to leave St John, since we have been reading from his gospel on the weekdays of Christmas.

On this Sunday of Year C we read the story of the Wedding Feast of Cana. As always with readings from St John, we take for granted that the passage is deeply symbolical, and so we can be very creative in our interpretation. By calling Jesus' action a 'sign' – the word this gospel always uses to refer to his miracles

– the text invites us to see it as a living lesson leading us to understand God's saving work in Jesus.

We celebrate God's work from two points of view: as its beneficiaries, and as those called to collaborate with him in bringing it to fulfillment.

We can identify three aspects of the story:
- the miracle;
- how Jesus came to be involved;
- the intercessory power of Mary.

1. The miracle of Cana is the transformation of water into 'the best wine'. What was colourless and bland becomes colourful and sparkling, a source of joy and energy.

Though we are free to apply the story to any experience of transformation, it is highly significant that the water was 'meant for the ablutions that are customary among the Jews'; this is a transformation of religion, therefore – it had become bland, self-centred, focused on personal purity, now it is renewed and brings joy into the world.

It is a common theme of the gospels that Jesus' mission was to transform the religion of his time and make it more human – the sabbath is for human beings, not human beings for the sabbath. In Jesus' parables the kingdom is often compared to a wedding feast; when the Pharisees complained that Jesus' disciples did not fast, he answered that 'the bridegroom was with them'; in contrast with John the Baptist, Jesus 'comes eating and drinking.'

Another significant aspect of the miracle is that Jesus starts with the water that was there. This is a 'sign' – the work of redemption, unlike creation, does not create out of nothing.

2. The way St John tells the story, Jesus chose to work the miracles as the conclusion of a personal journey in four stages:
  a) Mary draws his attention to the need;
  b) Jesus refuses to get involved on two counts,
     - 'Why turn to me?' (in the more common version, 'What is that to me and to you?')
     - 'My hour has not yet come'.
  c) Mary tells the servants to do whatever Jesus says;
  d) Jesus gets involved.

Scholars have offered different interpretations of Jesus' journey.

As always, personal experience is our most reliable guide. We can see the journey as the movement by which people of faith are led by God to enter into a new commitment, a new 'hour' of grace, requiring a higher degree of self-giving.

3. Again starting with experience, we can see Mary as 'the woman' – either within the human community or within each person. She is the compassionate one, sensitive to the needs of those around her, and sensitive also to the journey that Jesus must make, challenging him and yet leaving him free.

* * *

Lord, we thank you for times when, by a movement of grace,
we enter into a new level of commitment:
    - begin praying more contemplatively;
    - are reconciled with someone who has hurt us or our fami-
    lies;
    - join a movement working for social change;
    - enter a religious community;
    - leave a secure job in order to serve the poor.
It always seems to happen suddenly.
We are doing things as we always have,
relating with family, friends and fellow workers as before.
When we hear that the people around us have no wine
we see no reason why they should turn to us;
like Jesus, we say, 'My hour has not come yet.'
Then you send Mary into our lives,
someone who feels the pain of those around her,
someone who knows us so well that she perceives
that we are more ready to get involved than we realise.
She tells those around to trust us
and then leaves us to do things in our own way
and at our own time.
Through some mysterious change of heart,
which neither others nor we ourselves can explain,
we find ourselves taking charge of the situation
and answering the need,
transforming water into wine.
Your grace within us is revealed to others – and to ourselves.

'In Jerusalem, this holy city of three mighty religions, no one seems to have the faith to make the peaceful decision.' David Rudder, calypsonian

Lord, the different religions of the world
have as their special role
to preserve the vision of the world
as a great wedding feast where
- ancient enemies are reconciled,
- ethnic groups work in harmony,
- human beings and nature are one,
- there is no more dualism between humanity and divinity.
But so often, when we find ourselves in a situation of conflict,
our groups act as if this is not our concern.
Like the water jars at the wedding feast of Cana,
which were meant for the ablutions
that were customary among the Jews,
our observances become a matter of preserving our identity
and of keeping ourselves pure,
cleansing ourselves from what we consider
the contamination of the world around us.
We pray that you will send us religious leaders like Jesus
who will transform our faith into a source of joy and vitality,
so that the men and women of our time will experience
that the religions of the world have kept their best wine till now.

'A time will come when we will once again be called so to utter the Word of God that the world will be changed and renewed by it. It will be a new language, perhaps quite non-religious, but liberating and redeeming.' Dietrich Bonhoffer

Lord, the preaching of your Word in our church
has so lost its power that we are surprised
when our contemporaries turn to us in their need.
We pray that the hour of grace will come
when the water which our preaching has become
will be transformed into delightful refreshing wine.

'We must find the courage to leave our temples and enter into the temples of human experience, temples that are filled with human suffering.' Buddhist saying
Lord, the hour always comes for your church
when, like Jesus at the wedding feast of Cana,
we listen to the women among us
and respond to the needs of the world.

'Night is our diocese and silence is our ministry, poverty is our charity and helplessness our tongue-tied sermon.' Thomas Merton
Lord, give us the courage
to come before you like Mary before Jesus,
saying simply, 'They have no wine,' and leaving the rest to you.

'The days are coming when harvest will follow directly after ploughing, the treading of grapes soon after sowing, when the mountains will run with new wine and the hills all flow with it.' Amos 9:13
Lord, your will is that the whole world
should be a place of abundance for the whole human family.
Yet Mary's words to Jesus at the wedding feast of Cana
are echoing in many countries today.
Men and women have no wine to share with their families,
since the wine which nature provided for the festivals
has all gone,
plundered by the modern economy,
industrial estates and misdirected projects.
Forgive us that so often our church says to them,
'Why turn to us?'
We pray that like Jesus we will be moved to listen
to the pain of your people
so that the hour of grace may come
when we will work with them
to discover the untapped sources of abundance among them,
and from the water jars standing there
they will draw out gallons of the best wine,
they will see your glory and believe in you.

Third Sunday in Ordinary Time

Gospel reading: Luke 1:1-4; 4:14-21

¹*Seeing that many others have undertaken to draw up accounts of the events that have taken place among us, ²exactly as these were handed down to us by those who from the outset were eyewitnesses and ministers of the word ³I in my turn, after carefully going over the whole story from the beginning, have decided to write an account for you, Theophilus, ⁴so that your Excellency may learn how well founded the teaching is that you have received.*

¹⁴*Jesus, with the power of the spirit in him, returned to Galilee, and his reputation spread throughout the countryside. ¹⁵He taught in their synagogues and everyone praised him. ¹⁶He came to Nazara, where he had been brought up, and went into the synagogue on the sabbath day as he usually did. He stood up to read, ¹⁷and they handed him the scroll of the prophet Isaiah. Unrolling the scroll he found the place where it is written:*

¹⁸*'The spirit of the Lord has been given to me,*
for he has anointed me.
He has sent me to bring the good news to the poor,
to proclaim liberty to captives and to the blind new sight,
to set the downtrodden free,
¹⁹*to proclaim the Lord's year of favour.'*

²⁰*He then rolled up the scroll, gave it back to the assistant and sat down. And all eyes in the synagogue were fixed on him. ²¹Then he began to speak to them, 'This text is being fulfilled today even as you listen.'*

The reflection below is on the second part of the reading – verses 16 to 21 – a story of how Jesus read the Bible and how he wants us his followers to read it (and teach it).

Verses 16-17 and 20-21 explain the method; verses 18 and 19 give the text Jesus read.

As regards the method, we are free to interpret the passage as what happens to the church as a whole or to individual members. The biblical renewal of recent years was a matter of the whole church being handed the Bible (by an assistant) and invited to recognise it being fulfilled today.

We can also interpret the passage as reminding us of what happens when individuals get down to personal Bible meditation. In this case the passage is a living lesson on the lectio divina method.

If we go as far as drawing wisdom conclusions, we will learn something about how Bible teachers can guide people into experiencing what Jesus did – that their experience is not unique and therefore alienating, but the Bible is fulfilled in them. Good Bible teachers teach people how to recognise in their 'today' experience that they are in communion with their ancestors and with all God's people.

We can interpret 'the Bible text' as referring not merely to the Bible but to any ancestral text. The passage then becomes a teaching on good missionary method – the task of the missionary is to 'hand' ancestral texts to the people they are sent to, invite them to recognise that they are being 'fulfilled' in the church.

The passage also links the method with the content of the Isaiah text. It tells us (as always by appealing to our experience) that Bible reading correctly understood and practiced is an experience of liberation for those who are in any form of captivity – cultural, spiritual or psychological.

We must look for experiences which bring this out. In what way has the biblical renewal been an experience of liberation? For the church as a whole? For individuals? It has certainly been liberation from bondage to elitist, colonialist, racist and sexist thinking. To what extent has my Bible reading been a liberating experience for me, or for my community? If it has been, then who is the Bible teacher, spiritual guide, community leader, friend that we want to celebrate?

* * *

'Such is the force and power of the Word that it is the church's support and strength, imparting robustness to the faith of its daughters and sons and providing food for their souls, a pure and unfailing fount of spiritual life.' Vatican II, *Dei Verbum*

Lord, we thank you for the biblical renewal,
your precious gift to the church in our time.

- Other Christian churches initiated this great movement of the Spirit;

- it was recognised and welcomed by great popes like Leo
XIII and Pius XII,
- and was given further impetus by the Second Vatican
Council with this wonderful document on Divine Revelation.
We pray that a love for your Holy Scripture
may continue to grow in your church,
with the Liturgy of the Word as its source and summit,
so that the story of Jesus when he first returned to Nazareth
may be relived each week
in church communities all over the world,
wherever your people assemble on the sabbath
as they usually do, in their places of worship
– great cathedrals, parish churches and chapels
of religious houses, classrooms, community centres and homes,
or in the open air.
We pray that when celebrants stand up to read
and the book of readings is handed to them
they will open it with the utmost reverence
and accept with humble gratitude
whatever text they find written there,
read it clearly and deliberately,
conscious that your Spirit is being given to them
and they are being anointed
to transform this ancient writing into good news to the poor,
liberty to captives and new sight to the blind,
to recognise that our modern age,
for all its shortcomings, is a time of your favour.
When they have read the word,
may they maintain their reverence
as they close the book and hand it back to the assistant,
spend some moments in deep meditation,
aware that the eyes of all are fixed on them,
hungering and thirsting for a word of life,
and when eventually the time comes for them to begin to speak
may they present the Bible text not as an abstract message,
a story about the past to be remembered with nostalgia,
an impossible utopia that con only be dreamed of,
but being fulfilled among them even as they are listening.

Within the reality of their daily lives, their pains and their joys,
they will see your glorious story of grace triumphing over sin.

Lord, we pray that our church
may help men and women of every culture
to unroll the sacred scrolls of their tradition,
read attentively and reverently what they find written there,
sit down and meditate deeply on it
and recognise that this text is being fulfilled among them
as they listen.

Lord, our Western education system
sometimes contradicts the word of your prophets
   - brings bad news to the poor telling them that they deserve
   what they get.
   - plunges captives into deeper captivity,
   - keeps people blind so that they cannot see the opportunities
   for grace in their situations,
   - encourages the downtrodden to be resigned to their fate.
We pray that,
like Jesus returning to the place where he was brought up
and discovering his calling,
so we your church may return to our beginnings,
receive the Spirit you have sent us,
and the anointing with which we have been anointed,
and the oppressed people of our time
will hear us proclaim the good news
that they are born to be free
and a new year of favour will begin for them.

'My cell will be not one of stone or of wood, but of self-knowledge.'
St Catherine of Siena
Lord, when we find that our reputation
has spread throughout the countryside,
do not let us become pretentious
or lose the sense of who we really are.
Give us the grace to follow in the footsteps of Jesus
when he came to Nazara
where he had been brought up
so that we too will discover the truth of ourselves fulfilled in the
texts of Scripture.

'In your book all human beings are written.' Bruno of Seguin, medieval
monk and bishop
Lord, one of the great sufferings of people nowadays
is a sense of isolation,
the feeling that we are the first generation
to experience our problems;
and one of the great ways we follow in the footsteps of Jesus
is to help one another recognise
that the ancient scriptures are fulfilled in us.

Fourth Sunday in Ordinary Time

Gospel reading: Luke 4:21-30

21*Jesus began to speak in the synagogue: 'This text is being fulfilled today even as you listen.'* 22*And he won the approval of all, and they were astonished by the gracious words that came from his lips. They said, 'This is Joseph's son, surely?'* 23*But he replied, 'No doubt you will quote me the saying, "Physician, heal yourself" and tell me, "We have heard all that happened in Capernaum, do the same here in your own countryside".'* 24*And he went on, 'I tell you solemnly, no prophet is ever accepted in his own country.* 25*There were many widows in Israel, I can assure you, in Elijah's day, when heaven remained shut for three years and six months and a great famine raged throughout the land,* 26*but Elijah was not sent to any one of these; he was sent to a widow at Zarephath, a Sidonian town.* 27*And in the prophet Elisha's time there were many lepers in Israel, but none of these was cured, except the Syrian, Naaman.'*

28*When they heard this everyone in the synagogue was enraged.* 29*They sprang to their feet and hustled him out of the town; and they took him up to the brow of the hill their town was built on, intending to throw him down the cliff,* 30*but he slipped through the crowd and walked away.*

The incident related in today's gospel story is a precious moment of grace for the people of Nazareth, one that we too experience from time to time – Jesus invites them to stop hiding behind their false identity and come to the truth of themselves.

We all need to feel special; the problem is how we go about fulfilling that need. The easy – but false – way is to take the short cut of finding our 'specialness' in belonging to a group that considers itself superior to others. We find our 'specialness' in our sex, race, colour, ethnic origin, nationality, or from the fact that we are married, are 'old boys' or 'old girls' of some school, university graduates, have a job, or own our homes.

Today's reading reminds us that the same happens with religious groups. The people of Nazara, like the Jews in general, like members of churches, or of groups within them such as priests, religious and leaders of prayer groups, look on themselves as 'the chosen people'.

The basic fault in all these situations is to forget that being part of a group says nothing about our personal worth. If we settle for the group-identity we become complacent and stop facing the truth about ourselves.

The moment of grace comes when someone from our group sees through the cover up, starts mixing with outsiders, and declares that some of them are every bit as good as we are, perhaps even better. A good Catholic boy marries a girl from a different faith, and comes back to say that his in-laws are just as holy as members of his church. One of our own children, perhaps in a moment of anger, shows up our double standards and compares us unfavourably with our neighbours.

We think of those who refuse to play the racial game in politics, business or sport, and criticise members of their own religious or ethnic group. At the world level, Pope John Paul asks forgiveness for the sins of the church, Gandhi refers to the dalits as God's special children, Nelson Mandela forgives the former rulers of South Africa.

Our spontaneous reaction may be to be angry with those who break ranks. We brand them 'traitors'. Our anger is understandable. We are suddenly faced with the reality that we are not 'a master race', 'born to rule', 'chosen people'; we must take our place alongside people that we considered inferior, admit our failings, work hard for success.

In the church, all of us – priests, religious, laity – realise that we must 'work for our salvation with fear and trembling'.

The person moves on and leaves us to ponder this painful but very important moment of truth. Very gradually, over a period of months perhaps, the truth sets us free. Our anger turns to gratitude, we thank God that the Jesus-person he sent us did not flinch before our anger, but slipped away quietly leaving us to move from a false identity and find our true selves.

* * *

Lord, we thank you that every once in a way
you send us people like Jesus
who shock us by showing us that we have been hiding
behind the identity of the group we belong to.
They remind us of people who don't belong to our group,

whom you have blessed,
a humble widow who was visited by a great prophet,
the leader of a different religious group
whom you healed miraculously
while we were left with our diseases.
It is a painful lesson, especially when it comes
from someone within our own household,
and we exclaim, 'This is Joseph's son, surely,
what right has he to be teaching us?'
But it is a moment of grace;
we realise that we must stop looking down
on people of other ethnic groups,
of lesser education than ourselves;
we must join members of other churches,
religions and faiths, and unbelievers too,
in asking for your mercy and forgiveness.

Lord, you know that our first response is to become enraged
with those who tell us these home truths,
spring to our feet, hustle them out of our town,
take them up to the brow of the hill our church is built on,
intending to throw them down the cliff.
We thank you that the Jesus you sent us
slipped out of our grasp and walked away,
leaving us to ponder on the truth,
experience that the Bible was being fulfilled even as we listened,
and we eventually found life
from the gracious words that came from his lips.

Fifth Sunday in Ordinary Time

Gospel reading: Luke 5:1-11

¹Jesus was standing one day by the Lake of Gennesaret, with the crowd pressing round him listening to the word of God, ²when he caught sight of two boats close to the bank. The fishermen had gone out of them and were washing their nets. ³He got into one of the boats – it was Simon's - and asked him to put out a little from the shore. Then he sat down and taught the crowds from the boat.

⁴When he had finished speaking he said to Simon, 'Put out into the deep water and pay out your nets for a catch.' ⁵Master,' Simon replied 'we worked hard all night long and caught nothing, but if you say so, I will pay out the nets.' ⁶And when they had done this they netted such a huge number of fish that their nets began to tear, ⁷so they signalled to their companions in the other boat to come and help them; when they came, they filled the two boats to sinking point.

⁸When Simon Peter saw this he fell at the knees of Jesus saying, 'Leave me, Lord; I am a sinful man.' ⁹For he and all his companions were completely overcome by the catch they had made; ¹⁰so also were James and John, sons of Zebedee, who were Simon's partners. But Jesus said to Simon, 'Do not be afraid; from now on it is men you will catch.' ¹¹Then, bringing their boats back to land, they left everything and followed him.

The miraculous catch of fish was a historical event in the life of Jesus, but also a symbol of the deep conversion experiences which God grants us from time to time and which set us on a new course in our lives. These experiences usually occur at times when we feel we are stagnating – as spouses, parents, friends, church leaders, ministers, or managers in the work place. We are toiling all night and catching nothing.

Then one day God sends Jesus to us and he tells us to 'put out into deep water' – to move in a new, and frightening, direction. The message might come from a person or a sermon, a book, a television programme, a news item in the papers. Sometimes Jesus speaks to us from a negative experience – failure, rejection, falling into a sin we thought we would never commit, recognition that we are addicted to drugs or drink or power.

We each have our deep water we must put out into: be reconciled with someone we have refused to speak to for years; give up devotions we love and move to a more contemplative prayer; start working among the poor; get involved in community development; go back to school; join AA; do a Marriage Encounter weekend or a Life in the Spirit seminar. We put out objections like St Peter's: 'we have toiled all night,' 'what will happen if...,' 'we tried this before and it didn't work,' and so on. But we do it anyway and it works – relationships take on new life, classes or work-places become places of inspiration, our prayer life takes off – so much so that our problem now becomes how to cope with all we have to do: our nets begin to tear.

We feel overwhelmed: 'Leave me Lord, I am a sinner.' We who were totally bored now have a feeling of awe at the privilege of being spouse, parent, teacher in classroom or parish, or just to be a baptised Christian.

We know then that our lives can never be the same again: 'from now on it is men you will catch.' This must be interpreted correctly. God does not want us to go round trying to 'catch' people. The text means first getting involved with people not things, and secondly (according to the parable in Matthew 13:47 -50) that our mission in life is to lead one another into God's net, so that we can all be gathered into his kingdom. The Lord wants us from now on to care for people, help them to grow in self-esteem, move away from addictions, from abusive marriages – all the different ways in which we need to be brought closer to God and feel safe in his net.

This new consciousness means giving up things that we thought important. We do it cheerfully; we are 'not afraid' as we bring our boats back to land and without giving them a second thought, leave them there to follow the new way God has called us to.

* * *

Lord, we remember the day
when your son Jesus found us washing our nets,
discouraged since we were toiling all night
and catching nothing.
He said to us, 'Put out into deep water,'

and because he said so, we paid out our nets there.
We netted such a huge quantity of fish
that our nets began to tear
so that we signalled to companions in other boats
to come and help us
and even theirs were filled to sinking point.
We were completely overcome at the catch we made
and we fell on our knees in awe before you.
We knew then that we must make a change in our lives,
and focus on leading people into your net.
We brought our boats back to land
and left everything and followed Jesus.

Lord, our country is toiling all night
to solve our problems of crime,
domestic violence and unemployment and catching nothing.
Send us leaders like Jesus who will challenge us
to put out into the deep waters
of building a culture of love and pay out our nets there,
so that we may experience a miraculous catch,
and be so completely overcome
that we will fall at your knees saying,
'Leave us Lord, we are sinners.'
But we need not be afraid,
just bring those boats of selfishness to the land,
leave them there and follow you.

Sixth Sunday in Ordinary Time

Gospel reading: Luke 6:17, 20-26

17*Jesus came down with the Twelve and stopped at a piece of level ground where there was a large gathering of his disciples with a great crowd of people from all parts of Judaea and from Jerusalem and from the coastal region of Tyre and Sidon* 18*who had come to hear him and to be cured of their diseases. People tormented by unclean spirits were also cured* 19*and everyone in the crowd was trying to touch him because power came out of him that cured them all.*

20*Then fixing his eyes on his disciples he said: 'How happy are you who are poor: yours is the kingdom of God.* 21*Happy you who are hungry now: you shall be satisfied. Happy you who weep now: you shall laugh.* 22*Happy are you when people hate you, drive you out, abuse you, denounce your name as criminal, on account of the Son of Man.* 23*Rejoice when that day comes and dance for joy, for then your reward will be great in heaven. This was the way their ancestors treated the prophets.* 24*But alas for you who are rich: you are having your consolation now.* 25*Alas for you who have your fill now: you shall go hungry. Alas for you who laugh now: you shall mourn and weep.* 26*Alas for you when the world speaks well of you! This was the way their ancestors treated the false prophets.*

On this Sunday and the next, the gospel readings are extracts from St Luke's account of the 'sermon on the mount' which in *his* gospel should really be called the 'sermon on the plain'.

Jesus 'fixes his eyes' on us so that we can get to know him well and recognise his presence among us. His loving look is also a call to conversion so that we may be more like him.

'How happy are you who are poor!' This is not an abstract statement but a joyful exclamation at the greatness of the people he sees before him. It reminds us of another text which says that Jesus was 'filled with joy by the Holy Spirit' as he contemplated the wisdom of the little ones to whom God had revealed things which he had hidden from the 'learned and the clever'.

Jesus is so different from us. We tend to relate to the poor in a condescending way. Even when we love them we do it pityingly, we call them 'disadvantaged' or 'less fortunate than ourselves,' we want to 'do things for them', even to 'pray for them'.

Right through his life Jesus did the opposite. In the presence of those his society considered poor – the 'little ones,' 'sinners', 'tax-collectors and prostitutes' – he felt inspired, was filled with awe, and he told them so. 'Yours is the kingdom of God,' means that they are the ones who have the wisdom and the courage to make the kingdom a reality in the world.

We now see why St Luke says that Jesus 'stopped at a piece of level ground where there was a large gathering'. He didn't want to talk down to people; he would 'cure them of their diseases' by conversing with them at their level, entering into the greatness he saw in the midst of their poverty, hunger and tears.

He knew that like many poor people, they tended to look up to the ruling elites, the superstars of his time, with awe, perhaps with some envy, so he urged them not to be intimidated by their shallowness and false values. They must remain true to their own values and then their hunger would be satisfied and their weeping would become laughter and celebration.

There are 'great crowds of people' in our country, who need to be cured of many diseases – lack of self-confidence, fear of failure, narrow-mindedness. Not many are willing to do like Jesus, leave their homes and air-conditioned offices and come down to the level ground to 'fix their eyes on them', converse with them, enter into their greatness and their wisdom. Some pretend to do it, but not sincerely. They praise the poor but secretly look down on them, utter platitudes and do not 'exclaim' from the heart as Jesus does in this passage. A real challenge for us who are parents, community workers, teachers, church ministers.

St Luke says that Jesus' disciples were 'gathered with the crowd.' That is our church, a community of ordinary people, needing healing like the rest of humanity, 'sharing the joys and hopes, the grief and anguish of the people of our time, especially of those who are poor and afflicted' (Second Vatican Council).

* * *

Lord, we thank you for Jesus and people like him
who come down and stop at a piece of level ground,
where we and a great crowd of people are gathered
looking for a word of compassion

and to be cured of our diseases.
We thank you for those who reassure us that we are not bad,
that the kingdom of God is in our hands,
and even though right now we feel hunger,
and weep bitter tears,
we can be confident of the future.
We thank you for our ancestors in this country,
grandparents, mothers and fathers,
who taught us how to rejoice and dance for joy
even when people look down on us, drive us out,
abuse us, denounce our names as criminals.
Send the same Spirit of Wisdom
on the many people in our society who are very rich,
but that is all the consolation they have,
who seem to have their fill but are very hungry,
who outwardly are laughing
but when you get to know them are mourning and weeping,
who are well spoken of by the world
but are false prophets in fact.

Seventh Sunday in Ordinary Time

Gospel reading: Luke 6:27-38

27*Jesus said to his disciples: 'I say this to you who are listening: Love your enemies, do good to those who hate you,* 28*bless those who curse you, pray for those who treat you badly.* 29*To the man who slaps you on one cheek, present the other cheek too; to the man who takes your cloak from you, do not refuse your tunic.* 30*Give to everyone who asks you, and do not ask for your property back from the man who robs you.* 31*Treat others as you would like them to treat you.* 32*If you love those who love you, what thanks can you expect? Even sinners love those who love them.* 33*And if you do good to those who do good to you, what thanks can you expect? For even sinners do that much.* 34*And if you lend to those from whom you hope to receive, what thanks can you expect? Even sinners lend to sinners to get back the same amount.* 35*Instead, love your enemies and do good, and lend without any hope of return. You will have a great reward, and you will be sons of the Most High, for he himself is kind to the ungrateful and the wicked.* 36*Be compassionate as your Father is compassionate.* 37*Do not judge, and you will not be judged yourselves; do not condemn, and you will not be condemned yourselves; grant pardon, and you will be pardoned.* 38*Give, and there will be gifts for you: a full measure, pressed down, shaken together, and running over, will be poured into your lap; because the amount you measure out is the amount you will be given back.'*

We must meditate on this gospel reading as Jesus would want us to: not as a burdensome obligation (he condemned the Pharisees for imposing burdens on people), but as a celebration. 'Fixing his eyes' on us (last Sunday's reading), Jesus invites us to celebrate with him what is best in ourselves.

The language is poetical and dramatic, stirring up wonder in us at the wonderful thing that is generosity of spirit. People who are generous of spirit are able to go beyond the injustices they suffer – insults (the meaning of the slap on the cheek), dishonesty, cruelty – and hear a cry for help, the desperate search for love and respect, to be recognised as a person of worth.

Every once in a way God blesses our world with such people

– St Francis of Assisi in earlier times, Gandhi and Mother Teresa in our century. The passage reminds us that they are the 'sons and daughters of the Most High', who reveal new possibilities for humanity. Those of us who have met them in person remember it as a mystical experience.

We have known such people personally too – a father or mother, grandparent, aunt or uncle, a friend who mirrored for us the infinite compassion of God, brought sacredness to our homes, neighbourhoods, workplaces. We celebrate them with Jesus in this passage.

We celebrate our own greatness too, the fleeting moments when, as parents, teachers, friends, or church ministers, we found we had the capacity to rise above pettiness, desire for revenge and sectarianism, and reach out to others in love. We got a glimpse of the divine spark within us.

Jesus' way of teaching poses a challenge for us today. Nowadays people think that the most effective way to run a community is to inspire fear, pass laws, build more prisons, bring back the death penalty. As is commonly said, 'This is the only language they understand.'

Jesus used threats from time to time but it was always with a loving purpose. As the passage shows, he knew that the only way to get us to move forward is to meet us at the level where we will freely choose to be generous.

Love therefore is still the most powerful force in the world, in dealing with individuals as well as in building communities. The passage ends by reminding us how generosity of spirit brings out the best in people and leads to abundance for all.

We think of parents celebrating their golden anniversaries surrounded with love, reaping the rewards of their years of self-sacrifice.

This passage is also a teaching on economics. 'A full measure pressed down, shaken together and running over' is an image of an abundant crop of grain. Our world is crippled by shortages of food because agricultural policies are guided by selfishness and meanness. The passage tells us that a culture of love will bring about a world of abundance.

* * *

Lord, we thank you
for the sons and daughters of the Most High you send us
who touch us at the deepest level of ourselves.
They show us that we too can bless those who curse us,
pray for those who treat us badly,
reach out to those who have slapped us on the cheek,
offer our tunic to someone who had taken our cloak,
give whenever asked,
not ask for our property back when we are robbed,
treat others as we would like them to treat us,
lend without any hope of return.
They make us aware
that there is much more to us than our badness,
we are your sons and daughters,
kind to the ungrateful and the wicked, as you are.

We thank you for the extraordinary outpouring of love
at the deaths of Princess Diana and Mother Teresa.
They were not judgemental,
and in death no one passed judgment on them,
they who did not condemn were not condemned,
having pardoned much in their lifetimes,
they were now pardoned,
to them who had given generously, many gifts were given.

Lord, we pray that our leaders will inspire generosity of spirit
among those involved in agriculture,
so that there will be food for all –
a full measure, pressed down
and shaken together and running over
will be poured into the lap of humanity.

Eighth Sunday in Ordinary time

Gospel reading: Luke 6:39-45

*39Jesus told a parable to his disciples: 'Can one blind man guide another?
Surely both will fall into a pit? 40The disciple is not superior to his
teacher; the fully trained disciple will always be like his teacher. 41Why
do you observe the splinter in your brother's eye and never notice the
plank in your own? 42How can you say to your brother, 'Brother, let
me take out the splinter that is in your eye,' when you cannot see the
plank in your own? Hypocrite! Take the plank out of your own eye
first, and then you will see clearly enough to take out the splinter that
is in your brother's eye.*

*43There is no sound tree that produces rotten fruit, nor again a rotten
tree that produces sound fruit. 44For every tree can be told by its own
fruit: people do not pick figs from thorns, nor gather grapes from brambles. 45A good man draws what is good from the store of goodness in his
heart; a bad man draws what is bad from the store of badness. For a
man's words flow out of what fills his heart.'*

Good news: the fully trained disciple will be like his teacher. We,
Jesus' disciples, are called to be like him. Our doubts about ourselves, our feelings of inadequacy arise, in part, from the fact
that we forget that we did not choose him – he chose us; no one
can come to the Father unless the Father draws him. We have
been chosen, God has chosen to trust us; he believes that we can
be true disciples. This should be for us a source of great joy,
great humility, determination to become 'fully trained,' and self-
confident. If I am his disciple it is because he has chosen me and
trusts me to become like him. This is something to be celebrated
gratefully.

This will lead us to a new and deeper commitment: we must
learn to listen to Jesus and must be willing to learn from him,
otherwise we will only be like the blind man leading other blind
people and falling certainly into a pit. If we take discipleship se-
riously, we must commit ourselves to listening and learning and
being trained.

The fruit of prayer will be to reveal the plank in my own eye;
until I have meditated deeply on a gospel passage and experi-

enced conversion, I have nothing to say to anyone else. I would be a hypocrite were I to attempt doing so.

The test of the good disciple is in the fruit. People who came into contact with Jesus experienced healing, forgiveness, inner peace. Goodness wells out of the heart of the good disciple, who brings good news. The imagery is very dramatic – the thorns and brambles and rotten fruit. Notice too that what matters is what 'fills the heart', not scholarly knowledge and cleverness. Good fruit – action – will grow out of commitment at the heart level, not willful intellectual determination with clenched teeth.

This passage can be read in the context of last week's reading, as four parables, four concrete applications of the two central principles stated in last week's passage – loving our enemies and sharing our possessions with the poor:
- verse 39: enlightened leadership;
- verse 40: trained disciples;
- verses 41-42: hypocrisy in correcting others;
- verses 43-45: action must flow from faith, from inner conviction.

Using words for good rather than for evil is a very concrete application which we might want to reflect on. There are many ways in which we can make a destructive use of words, forgetting that they have tremendous power.

* * *

'Spiritual poverty clings to what is his own and nothing clings to it.'
Meister Eckhart
Lord, we know that there are many blind people in our world
who are at present leading others
who are themselves very blind.
We know that they must both end up in the one place only.
They will fall into a terrible pit, where they will hurt themselves
and also those others who let themselves be guided by them
to a safe place.

'I am disarmed of the will to overcome, to justify myself at the expense of others. I am no longer on the alert, jealously guarding my riches.'
Patriarch Athenagoras
Lord, we as your disciples cannot be superior

to our great and noble teacher
with his own greatness and goodness.
Remind us that we are all fully trained disciples
and so we will only have the power to help others, as you did,
to get to the brightness and greatness of God's presence
and to live there for ever.

Lord, forgive us
that we look for the splinter in our brother's or sister's eye
and so do not notice that there is a plank in our own.
Remind us Lord, that we cannot say to our brother or sister,
'Let me take the splinter that is in your eye,'
and never even notice that there is a plank in ours.
Remind us, Lord, how hypocritical we are,
help us to take the plank from our own eye first
and then we will see clearly enough
to take out the splinter that is in our brother's or sister's eye.

*'Whether it is the surface of Scripture or the material form of nature,
both serve to clothe the Christ. They are two veils that mask the radiance of the faith and at the same time reflect his beauty.'* John Scotus
Eriugenus
Lord, remind us that no sound tree ever produces rotten fruit,
and a rotten tree can only produce rotten fruit.
Remind us that every tree can be told by its own fruit,
that people do not pick figs from thorns
nor gather grapes from brambles.

*'Many of those who reject the Word of God, reject it because the way we
say it is utterly meaningless to them. They know the dimension of the
eternal but they cannot accept our names for it. If we want them as free
persons, we must know they have received a word from the Lord.'* Paul
Tillich
Lord, remind us that people draw what is good
from what is a store of goodness in their hearts.
A bad man draws what is bad from his store of badness.
A person's words will naturally flow out
from what fills their heart.

Ninth Sunday in Ordinary Time

Gospel reading: Luke 7:1-10

[1]*When he came to the end of all he wanted the people to hear, Jesus went into Capernaum.* [2]*A centurion there had a servant, a favourite of his, who was sick and near death.* [3]*Having heard about Jesus he sent some Jewish elders to him to ask him to come and heal his servant.* [4]*When they came to Jesus they pleaded earnestly with him. 'He deserves this of you' they said* [5]*'because he is friendly towards our people; in fact, he is the one who built the synagogue.'* [6]*So Jesus went with them, and was not very far from the house when the centurion sent word to him by some friends: 'Sir,' he said 'do not put yourself to trouble; because I am not worthy to have you under my roof;* [7]*and for this same reason I did not presume to come to you myself; but give the word and let my servant be cured.* [8]*For I am under authority myself, and have soldiers under me; and I say to one man: Go, and he goes; to another: Come here, and he comes; to my servant: Do this, and he does it.'* [9]*When Jesus heard these words he was astonished at him and, turning round, said to the crowd following him, 'I tell you, not even in Israel have I found faith like this.'* [10]*And when the messengers got back to the house they found the servant in perfect health.*

The gospel passage for this Sunday has a brief introduction in verse 1. You might like to meditate on it by itself. What does it tell you about the kind of teacher Jesus was?

Verses 2 to 10 give us the main story in one continuous flow. You can read it from two points of view – a story of the centurion, or a story of Jesus.

The centurion is one of the most attractive characters in the gospels and it should be easy for you to identify with him. He is a person who knows power and takes delight in exercising it (verse 8), but at this moment in his life he knows that all he can do is to trust, and he gives himself willingly and fully to that experience. Of course, there was always a tender side to his character; he looked on one of his servants as his 'favourite', and he had made friends with the Jewish leaders.

Jesus is the great leader and teacher, confident in himself as he goes ahead of the crowd, and yet humbly grateful at this un-

expected manifestation of God's grace. Can we not say that
Jesus and the centurion have a lot in common?

* * *

Lord, we who are priests or ministers in the church,
we do a lot of teaching.
Help us to know, like Jesus did,
when we have to come to the end of all we want people to hear
and must now go out to meet them in their life situations,
because there are centurions there waiting for us,
not the kind of people who come to hear us teach,
but they are in anguish
because their dear ones need to be healed.

*'The ultimate measure of man is not where he stands in moments of
comfort but where he stands at times of challenge and controversy.'*
Martin Luther King
Lord, there are times
when we experience ourselves in control of our lives:
   - things are going well in our family, at work and in our personal relationships;
   - we are telling people to go and they go, others to come and
   they come, others again to do this and they do it;
   - we are in a position to be friendly to strangers and to do
   them favours.
But there always seems to come another kind of time
when our secure world collapses:
   - we lose our self confidence so that we cannot presume to
   come to others ourselves;
   - we don't want anyone to come and see us as we are.
This can be a time of grace
when we experience the healing power of others
and find within ourselves a faith we never knew we had.

Lord, you lead people along strange ways.
We remember today someone we knew,
a powerful, domineering person,
always telling others to go and they went,
to do this and sure enough they did it.

Then one day he fell sick and was near death.
We remember how touching it was to see him so humble,
not wanting to put others to any trouble,
or presuming to ask them to come to his house.
We were astonished as we had never found faith like this before.

*'In prayer we stand alone before God in our nothingness, without
explanation, without theories, completely dependent upon his providential care, in dire need of the gift of his grace, his mercy and the light
of faith.'* Thomas Merton
Lord, we thank you for moments of deep prayer.
At those moments we know that we are in need of healing.
Others may speak highly of us
and can recount all kinds of good things we have done,
but we do not feel there is anything in us
that would make us worthy of your favour
and we would think it presumptuous
for us to say anything to you at all.
At the same time we feel
an overwhelming trust in your love and power,
and we know that you only have to give one word
for us to be restored to full health
Thank you, Lord.

Lord, we church people tend to become narrow-minded,
thinking that you give your grace only to us.
We even resent it when we hear of spiritual people
who belong to other churches,
follow other religions or follow no religion at all.
We pray that we may be open, like Jesus,
glad like he was to confess our astonishment
when we are touched by those who do not belong to us,
and to say openly to the crowds who follow
that we have not found faith like this within our church.

Tenth Sunday in Ordinary Time

Gospel reading: Luke 7:11-17

¹¹*Soon afterwards, Jesus went to a town called Nain, accompanied by his disciples and a great number of people.* ¹²*When he was near the gate of the town, it happened that a dead man was being carried out for burial, the only son of his mother, and she a widow. And a considerable number of townspeople were with her.* ¹³*When the Lord saw her he felt sorry for her. 'Do not cry' he said.* ¹⁴*Then he went up and put his hand on the bier and the bearers stood still, and he said, 'Young man, I tell you to get up.'* ¹⁵*And the dead man sat up and began to talk, and Jesus gave him to his mother.* ¹⁶*Everyone was filled with awe and praised God saying, 'A great prophet has appeared among us; God has visited his people.'* ¹⁷*And this opinion of him spread throughout Judaea and all over the countryside.*

Like last Sunday's gospel reading, this one is a continuous story. It is more complex, however, in that there are several characters we can identify with.

The only active person is Jesus, so that the passage invites us to 'fix our eyes on him' (Heb 12:2). The story lays stress on his compassion (verse 13) as the source of his power to bring the man back to life. Note that the object of Jesus' compassion is not the dead man but the mother.

The mother was a widow and this was her only son. She is therefore a symbol of the totally defenceless person; all her sources of security have been lost.

The bearers are those who are taking someone out for burial when in fact he can still be restored to life through the power of compassion.

The crowd, referred to in the passage as 'everyone', are people in general who experience the presence of God through the work of Jesus.

* * *

Lord, so often we write off people;
- alcoholics and drug addicts;
- delinquent children;
- vagrants and those we call unemployable.
We thank you for the times that you sent Jesus into our town
accompanied by his disciples and a large number of people:
- Alcoholics Anonymous
- the Vincent de Paul Society
- communities such as L'Arche, Emmanuel, Living Water
and Zion;
- those who work in rehabilitation centres.
Strong in their compassion they made us stand still,
got those whom we were carrying out for burial to stand up
and begin to speak for themselves,
and gave them back to their mothers
so that we were filled with awe
and praised you for having visited your people.

Lord, there is a lot of despair in many countries today.
There was a time when these people dreamt of better days
and a new world they would create.
Today, like the widow in the gospel story,
they are seeing these dreams being carried out for burial.
We pray that your church, like Jesus,
may feel compassion for these people
and give them back their hopes for a glorious future.

*'It strikes me that the reason why the world is not very much interested
in the church is essentially because the church is not really interested
in Christ.'* A priest at the Annual Conference of Priests of England and Wales
Lord, we sometimes feel
that the church is losing its influence in the world
and we conclude that we need more TV programmes,
more learned teaching, or more organisations.
But if people see the church living the story of Jesus,
going into towns, feeling compassion for those who mourn,
telling them not to cry,
and giving them back their reason for living,
then they will be filled with awe,

they will know that a great prophet has appeared among them,
and this opinion of the church will spread
throughout the towns and all over the countryside.

'All over the world I have found small groups who are building a new world in the shell of the one crumbling around us.' Maisie Ward
Lord, there are many things happening in the world today
that fill us with apprehension:
    - thousands of abortions carried out every day;
    - famine alongside an abundance of food;
    - children dying of disease even though medicines are available.
It is as if our civilisation is being carried out for burial.
Yet if we look closely we will see that Jesus is alive,
accompanied by his disciples and a great number of people
who are not his disciples but live according to his values:
    - organisations like OXFAM that are always there to provide relief in disaster areas;
    - the co-operative movement;
    - Amnesty International protecting the rights of those jailed unjustly.
They are putting their hands on the bier
so that the bearers stand still.
They are giving life back to our world.

Lord, we pray for political leaders.
They very easily become isolated from people
as they get caught up with problems at the national level.
We pray that like Jesus
they may go into the towns and villages of their country,
together with great numbers of people who surround them,
and there see the little people who are weeping
at the loss of what was most precious to them,
and not only feel pity for them,
but effectively bring joy back to their lives,
so that the country can feel blessed again.

Lord, when Jesus died on the cross
humanity's only hope was gone.
By raising him from the dead
you told us not to cry and gave him back to us.

Lord, we pray for countries that are experiencing violence
– Iraq, Turkey, Northern Ireland, Zimbabwe, Palestine, Israel.
So many of their young people are being carried out for burial.
Raise up among them people like Jesus
who will stop the violence
and the young people will have reason to live again.

Eleventh Sunday in Ordinary Time

Gospel reading: Luke 7:36-50

36*One of the Pharisees invited Jesus to a meal. When he arrived at the Pharisee's house and took his place at table,* 37*a woman came in, who had a bad name in the town. She had heard he was dining with the Pharisee and had brought with her an alabaster jar of ointment.* 38*She waited behind him at his feet, weeping, and her tears fell on his feet, and she wiped them away with her hair; then she covered his feet with kisses and anointed them with the ointment.*

39*When the Pharisee who had invited him saw this, he said to himself, 'If this man were a prophet, he would know who this woman is that is touching him and what a bad name she has.'* 40*Then Jesus took him up and said, 'Simon, I have something to say to you.' 'Speak, Master' was the reply.* 41*There was once a creditor who had two men in his debt; one owed him five hundred denarii, the other fifty.* 42*They were unable to pay, so he pardoned them both. Which of them will love him more?'* 43*'The one who was pardoned more, I suppose' answered Simon. Jesus said, 'You are right.'* 44*Then he turned to the woman. 'Simon,' he said 'you see this woman? I came into your house, and you poured no water over my feet, but she has poured out her tears over my feet and wiped them away with her hair.* 45*You gave me no kiss, but she has been covering my feet with kisses ever since I came in.* 46*You did not anoint my head with oil, but she has anointed my feet with ointment.* 47*For this reason I tell you that her sins, her many sins, must have been forgiven her, or she would not have shown such great love. It is the man who is forgiven little who shows little love.'*

48*Then he said to her, 'Your sins are forgiven.'* 49*Those who were with him at table began to say to themselves, 'Who is this man, that he even forgives sins?'* 50*But he said to the woman, 'Your faith has saved you; go in peace.'*

Once again, as in the last two Sundays, we see Jesus relating with people. This time the passage is much more complex.

First of all, there are really two stories:

- Jesus relates with the Pharisee in verses 39 to 47.

- Jesus relates with the woman in verses 36 to 38 and then again in verses 48 and 50.

St Luke evidently intended the two stories to shed light on each other, but they can also be taken separately.

In either story you can focus on Jesus, noting how he treats each of the two people differently, according to their needs, but being compassionate and respectful to both.

You can identify with the Pharisee, noting his good points as well as the bad ones, making sure you don't read it self-righteously, but discovering yourself in him.

The woman symbolises all outcasts, those who 'have a bad name in town' for any reason whatsoever.

The parable in verse 41 can stand on its own and you may find that it touches you.

Verse 49 introduces a group of people 'with Jesus at table'; you may find that you identify with them, or with the way Jesus relates with them in verse 50.

* * *

'Of all mankind's needs, the most persistent, terrible and demanding is that which springs from the inescapable fact of sin and the need for forgiveness and redemption. This, first and last, is what priestly ministry is all about.' Norman Goodall

Lord, it happened in the past
that church leaders put too much stress on sin,
so that people were overly burdened by feelings of guilt.
As a result, today priests have gone to the other extreme
and do not allow us to make the painful journey to repentance.
Teach them to be like Jesus, to remain silent and respectful
as we wait humbly in the background, weeping for our sins:
    - sins of abortion;
    - how we have maltreated members of our family;
    - our jealousy of those who succeed where we have failed.
It is the only way we can know that our sins are forgiven,
that deeper than our sinfulness there is a faith which saves us
and that we can go in peace.

'Women are more linked than men to the soul of the world, to the primary, elemental forces. Masculine culture is too rational, too far from the immediate mysteries of cosmic life and it returns to it through women.' Nicolas Berdyaev

Lord, we thank you for the woman in today's gospel story,
and we thank you that Jesus defended her against the Pharisee.
We pray that our church leaders may do the same
for women in the world today.

Lord, in the church today
we have a way of categorising certain people as sinners.
We treat them with condescension
and speak of 'praying for their conversion'.
But this is not the way of Jesus.
When people came to him who had a bad name
in their communities
he welcomed them with respect, thanked them for their love,
proposed them as models for those who sat at table with him,
and assured them that it was their own faith
that had saved them.

'No one is so poor that they cannot give, and no one so rich that they cannot receive.' Helder Camara

Lord, give to your church the wisdom of Jesus,
that like him we may speak the right word to every group –
to those who are complacent like the Pharisee,
a word of challenge,
inviting them to discover their lack of humanity;
to those who are treated as outcasts,
like the woman in this story,
a word of encouragement and of healing.

Lord, in life we receive countless lessons that leave us unmoved.
But every once in a way you send us someone like Jesus,
one of our parents or relatives, a teacher, a spiritual guide.
They walk with us in our search for the truth;
'I have something to say to you' they tell us,
and then they wait for us to ask them before they continue.
They tell us stories, and let us discover for ourselves

the lesson they want us to draw,
assuring us then that we were right.
Thank you, Lord, for those teachers.

Lord, when we come to positions of authority in a community,
whether in the State or in the church,
we soon become cold and business-like
in our relationships with people.
We no longer welcome them warmly
or show them signs of affection.
It is because we are complacent.
But you always seem to send us some Jesus
who reminds us of the many things
people have had to pardon us
so that we could get where we now are.

Lord, there is within each one of us a sinful person
waiting in the shadows
and needing to be recognised and accepted.
Do not let the Pharisee in us repress that part of ourselves
as if good people should not let themselves be touched by sin.

Lord, truly kind people have an extraordinary power.
We who live with them are constantly amazed
at how they can make others experience
that their sins are forgiven.
Such people are the presence of Jesus with us.

Twelfth Sunday in Ordinary Time

Gospel reading: Luke 9:18-24

18*One day when Jesus was praying alone in the presence of his disciples, he put this question to them, 'Who do the crowds say I am?'* 19*And they answered, 'John the Baptist; others Elijah; and others say one of the ancient prophets come back to life.'* 20*'But you,' he said, 'who do you say I am?' It was Peter who spoke up. 'The Christ of God,' he said.* 21*But he gave them strict orders not to tell anyone anything about this.* 22*'The Son of Man,' he said, 'is destined to suffer grievously, to be rejected by the elders and chief priests and scribes and to be put to death, and to be raised up on the third day.'* 23*Then to all he said, 'If anyone wants to be a follower of mine, let him renounce himself and take up his cross every day and follow me.* 24*For anyone who wants to save his life will lose it; but anyone who loses his life for my sake, that man will save it.'*

Today's gospel reading is clearly divided into sections. In your meditation, start with one alone, although you may eventually find a connection between the different sections.

In verses 18 to 21 Jesus puts to his disciples the deepest and most sacred question that we can ask one another: 'Who do you say I am?' Identify with Jesus doing the asking, or with the disciples being asked. You can then concentrate either on the content of Peter's answer or on the way Jesus asked the question, e.g. why did he ask it the way he did, or why at this particular moment of his life.

In verse 22 Jesus says clearly that he knows the difficulties that his chosen path will bring him, and at the same time he is confident that he will eventually be victorious.

In verses 23 and 24 we have two of the most famous sayings of Jesus. In meditating on such paradoxical sayings, you must let yourself make a journey into the paradox, identifying with each part of the saying, and feeling that they are contradictory, but eventually discovering that they are not really so, and in the process entering into a new insight that touches you deeply. You might also ask yourself why is Jesus giving that kind of teaching today, to you personally or to the world.

Lord, people today think they can know themselves
through objective tests
that can be bought in a store and 'administered' by strangers.
But, as Jesus taught us, the question 'Who am I?' is a sacred one.
Others can help us only if they have walked with us for years,
if we have been alone with them for long hours
and they have prayed with us.
And when they have helped us it will be something so personal
that we will not want them to tell anyone about it.

Lord, we remember with gratitude
a retreat we made with some companions.
We remember how after those days
we knew them so much better,
partly because we had shared deeply,
but more from the mere fact
that they had prayed alone in our presence.
Before that retreat, we – like 'the crowds' –
had put them into categories according to their age,
race or social class,
or as other people we had known
who had come back to life in them.
Now we looked on them with reverence,
seeing them as unique individuals,
your own specially anointed ones.

Lord, forgive us that we want to be known as 'prophets'
or 'the presence of God in the world' or 'light of the world'.
Teach us to be humble like Jesus,
so that when people give us these titles
we will give them strict orders
not to tell anyone anything about this.

*'There is no way on this earth that you can say yes to human dignity
and know that you will be spared any kind of sacrifice.'* Cesar Chavez
Lord, once we give ourselves to a noble cause
there comes a time as it did for Jesus when we know for certain
that we are destined to suffer grievously,
that we will be rejected by people who have been our teachers,

and others whom we looked upon as holy and learned,
and that we will be defeated many times.
But deep down within us
we know too that we will always start again.

'In Caribbean politics, the moon is promised by politicians, and democracy consists in making a choice between competing sets of promises which are dangled temptingly every four or five years.' Michael Manley
Lord, we pray for our political leaders,
that they may be more like Jesus,
that they will respect us sufficiently to tell us honestly
that we must renounce our natural desire
for easy solutions to our problems,
and that we must take up every day
the burden of solving these problems from our own resources.
But of course they must also be like Jesus
in setting the example by doing this themselves.

Lord, it is one of the marks of Western civilisation today
that we need to be superior to others
in order to establish our identity:
    - men humiliate women to prove their masculinity;
    - nations arm themselves to the teeth to gain the respect of
    other nations;
    - as a church, we prove others false so that we can call ourselves true.
Send us teachers like Jesus to remind us
that we can never find our true vocation
by concentrating on ourselves,
but if we serve others after his example
you can lead us to our true selves.

'If today's flourishing civilisations remain selfishly wrapped up in themselves, they could easily place their highest values in jeopardy, sacrificing their will to be great to the desire to possess more.' Pope Paul VI
Lord, we thank you that the popes
are reaching nations with the message of Jesus
that if they want to save their true greatness
they must be willing to give up
some of their power and security.

Thirteenth Sunday in Ordinary Time

Gospel reading: Luke 9:51-62

51Now as the time drew near for him to be taken up to heaven, he resolutely took the road for Jerusalem 52and sent messengers ahead of him. These set out, and they went into a Samaritan village to make preparations for him, 53but the people would not receive him because he was making his way to Jerusalem. 54Seeing this, the disciples James and John said, 'Lord, do you want us to call down fire from heaven to burn them up?' 55But he turned and rebuked them, 56and they went off to another village. 57As they travelled along they met a man on the road who said to them, 'I will follow you wherever you go.' 58Jesus answered, 'Foxes have holes and the birds of the air have nests, but the Son of Man has nowhere to lay his head.' 59Another to whom he said, 'Follow me,' replied, 'Let me go and bury my father first.' 60But he answered, 'Leave the dead to bury their dead; your duty is to go and spread the news of the kingdom of God.' 61Another said, 'I will follow you, sir, but first let me go and say good-bye to my people at home.' 62Jesus said to him, 'Once the hand is laid on the plough, no one who looks back is fit for the kingdom of God.'

Today's gospel reading is divided into sections, and the general theme of commitment is running through them all.

In verses 51 to 56, Jesus is presented as a model of commitment; in 57 to 62, he gives three teachings which concretise in dramatic form the implications of a commitment.

In your meditation, feel free to draw on any experience of commitment which is deep and leads to spiritual growth.

In verses 51 to 56, St Luke shows us Jesus reaching a new level of clarity in his life. The result as shown in this incident is a combination of resoluteness and compassion; your meditation will reveal to you how true to life this is. The attitude of the two disciples is meant to contrast with that of Jesus; ask yourself, what made the difference between them?

In verses 57 and 58, the man on the road is asking Jesus to point out a definite place where he can lead him.

Jesus' response to the two people in verses 59 to 62 will seem harsh at first reading. Let your meditation remind you of great people who have touched your life and have made those kinds of demands on people; in that way you will understand what these responses tell us about the teaching of Jesus.

You might like to remain simply with the metaphor in verse 62 of laying one's hand on the plough and not turning back.

* * *

Lord, we think today of those who have just learnt
that they are suffering from an incurable disease.
Now they know that the time has drawn near
when they are to be taken to heaven,
may they resolutely take the road for Jerusalem.

'Make us know the shortness of our life, that we may gain wisdom of heart.' Psalm 90
Lord, we often find that
when we have resolutely taken some road
    - standing up against discrimination in our community,
    - deciding to forgive a long-standing hurt,
    - dedicating ourselves to the service of the poor,
we quickly become intolerant of those who disagree with us.
But if we keep in mind that the time is always drawing near
for us to be taken up to heaven, it makes us more compassionate,
so that when we send messengers ahead of us
and people will not receive them
because of where we are making for,
we do not call down fire from heaven to burn them up,
but merely go off to another village.

'In our inner journey there always remains something more to be given up, some new depth of God to be sounded, some deeper understanding of ourselves and the world.' Cyprian Smith OSB
Lord, how true it is that
when we are searching for union with you,
we can never remain still,
foxes may have holes and birds of the air nests,
but there is no place where we can lay our heads.

'For Christians, every place is a homeland and every homeland is a foreign land.' 2nd century writer

Lord, never let us, as a church, deceive our members
that we can lead them somewhere
where they can be permanently safe:
- a political or economic system that we won't need to question;
- a philosophy which will answer all our questions;
- a way of understanding the message of Jesus which gives the whole truth of his message.

Teach us to say frankly, as Jesus did,
that foxes have holes where they can lie down and rest,
birds of the air have their nests which they can call home,
but for us it is a constant search for where you want us to be.

'Once I committed myself to the Way, the word 'courage' lost its meaning, since nothing could be taken from me.' Dag Hammarskjold

Lord, how sweet and gentle is the moment of commitment.
No one has to tell us, we just know we are there.
Old fears have been laid to rest so completely
that we don't have to worry about burying them,
past attachments have faded away
so that we don't want to spend any time
saying good-bye to them,
our hands are laid on the plough
and to look back would be false to ourselves.

Lord, our societies are still torn by ideological conflicts
that are leading nowhere:
capitalism or communism, aligned or non-aligned, first, second or third world.
Send us leaders who will be straightforward like Jesus,
showing our people that
if we spend time laying these problems to rest,
we will be like dead people burying the dead,
whereas our duty is to go out and spread the news
that a new civilisation is being born and we can be part of it.

Fourteenth Sunday in Ordinary Time

Gospel text: Luke 10:1-12,17-20

¹*The Lord appointed seventy-two others and sent them out ahead of him, in pairs, to all the towns and places he himself was to visit.* ²*He said to them, 'The harvest is rich but the labourers are few, so ask the Lord of the harvest to send labourers to his harvest.* ³*Start off now, but remember, I am sending you out like lambs among wolves.* ⁴*Carry no purse, no haversack, no sandals. Salute no one on the road.* ⁵*Whatever house you go into, let your first words be, 'Peace to this house!'* ⁶*And if a man of peace lives there, your peace will go and rest on him; if not, it will come back to you.* ⁷*Stay in the same house, taking what food and drink they have to offer, for the labourer deserves his wages; do not move from house to house.* ⁸*Whenever you go into a town where they make you welcome, eat what is set before you.* ⁹*Cure those in it who are sick, and say, 'The kingdom of God is very near to you.'* ¹⁰*But whenever you enter a town and they do not make you welcome, go out into its streets and say,* ¹¹*'We wipe off the very dust of your town that clings to our feet, and leave it with you. Yet be sure of this: the kingdom of God is very near.'* ¹²*I tell you, on that day it will not go as hard with Sodom as with that town.*

¹⁷*The seventy-two came back rejoicing. 'Lord,' they said, 'even the devils submit to us when we use your name.'* ¹⁸*He said to them, 'I watched Satan fall like lightning from heaven.* ¹⁹*Yes, I have given you power to tread underfoot serpents and scorpions and the whole strength of the enemy; nothing shall ever hurt you.* ²⁰*Yet do not rejoice that the spirits submit to you; rejoice rather that your names are written in heaven.'*

In order to make a fruitful meditation on this passage, we must set ourselves some guidelines.

The first is that the seventy-two sent out by Jesus to go 'ahead of him to all the towns and places he himself was to visit' represent all of us in our different vocations. As spouses, parents, teachers, ministers in the church community, friends, spiritual guides, political or civic leaders, we open the way for others to meet God, 'go ahead of him'. Jesus' instructions can help us become life-giving in our deep relationships.

The second is that we must not read the passage in a moralising way, as if it is imposing a burden on us. Like all Bible passages, it invites us to celebrate with joy, humility and gratitude those, including ourselves, who have lived Jesus' instructions in practice. We have also failed to live them out of course, and from that perspective, the passage calls us, in communion with the whole church and all humanity, to conversion and repentance.

Thirdly we must enter into the highly imaginative language of the passage, allowing it to touch us even as it speaks to our reality. Two mistakes are to be avoided therefore: to 'interpret' the language so rationally that it no longer speaks to our emotions; to romanticise the passage so that it is not connected to real life.

The image of approaching people as a 'rich harvest' (the same as telling them, 'the kingdom of God is very near to you') is very touching and radical, but must be correctly interpreted. It speaks of approaching others not as objects of pity, but in admiration, aware of how much we can learn from them.

The attitude is especially important for missionaries and all who work in transcultural situations. Unfortunately it has not been the most common approach among church workers, neither in the past nor today.

There is an important message for those who hold leadership positions at local and national level. So often they don't trust the creativity of their communities.

Verses 4 and 5 evoke very dramatically the process of discarding prejudices, necessary if we are to meet people in their reality as a rich harvest.

'Lambs among wolves' tells us of the simplicity (to be distinguished from naïveté) this requires. It is the same as being 'poor in spirit.' 'No purse, no haversack, no sandals' means getting rid of mental baggage, especially cultural; 'salute no one on the road' is not deciding beforehand who we are going to admire.

Verse 6 reminds us that we must be free in ourselves, if our relationships are to be life-giving. Knowing that if our peace is rejected, it will 'come back to us' saves us from being co-dependent.

Verses 7 and 8, 'stay in the same house,' and 'eat what is set before you,' warn against giving ourselves half-heartedly and keeping an eye out for more attractive relationships.

Verses 10 and 11 raise the crucial issue of how to deal with rejection. Experience teaches that rejection brings out the baser motives which lurk beneath even our noble relationships. 'Wiping the dust off our feet' is a powerful description of the inner freedom by which we can move on to new commitments.

The basis of this inner freedom is to 'be sure that the kingdom of God is very near.'

* * *

Lord, we thank you for the people you send out ahead of you
to all the towns and places you yourself are to visit:
- by loving their children parents open them up to your unconditional love,
- spouses lift each other to a new plane of trustfulness,
- good neighbours bring the hope of new possibilities to a neighbourhood,
- those weighed down by troubles feel a surge of energy within them as they experience the care of friends or the listening ear of their spiritual guides,
- societies are inspired by their leaders,
- men and women like Mother Teresa, Mandela and Gandhi show the world humanity's potential for greatness.
We thank you
that Jesus' instructions are fulfilled in such people.
We note how he sends them in pairs,
males and females complementing one another,
male and female elements combined within each of them.
Whereas we tend to approach people in need
- as problems that we must solve,
- as less fortunate than ourselves and to be pitied,
- as helpless unless we rescue them,
they see in others, whatever their condition,
an abundant harvest waiting to be reaped;
if there is a problem, it is that there are too few labourers
and they must ask the Lord of the harvest
to send others to reap with them.

Lord we thank you for those who came to us
with openness, who did not
- try to bring us to their point of view
- prove that we were wrong

- insist that their way was the only one.
Like Jesus, they were humble and trusting
like lambs among wolves.

Lord we thank you for the great missionaries of the church,
who came to other cultures without baggage,
without ambition or power-seeking,
or looking to found an empire.
They carried no purse, no haversack, no sandals,
and had no pre-conceived ideas
on who they would salute on the road.

We pray that when we give our peace to others,
we will do so unreservedly,
not overly concerned about whether or not we will succeed,
trusting that if they are people of peace,
our peace will rest on them,
and if they are not,
we will not feel that we have wasted our energy,
since our peace will come back to us.

Forgive us, Lord, that we spend so much time regretting
that those to whom you send us
do not live up to our expectations,
so that we end up moving from house to house,
if only in our minds.
Teach us to be life-giving wherever we find ourselves,
staying in the same house,
taking whatever food and drink are offered us,
eating what is set before us.

Lord, when rejection by those we serve weighs us down
so that we don't have the energy to make a new start,
it tells us that our service
was really a way of affirming ourselves.
We pray that whenever we enter a town
and they do not make us welcome,
we will be able to go out into its streets,
say that we wipe off the very dust of the town

that clings to our feet
and leave it with them
while we move on to other places and people.
What will keep us free from resentment and bitterness
is knowing that your kingdom is very near.

Fifteenth Sunday in Ordinary Time

Gospel reading: Luke 10:25-37

25There was a lawyer who, to disconcert Jesus, stood up and said to him, 'Master, what must I do to inherit eternal life?' 26He said to him, 'What is written in the Law? What do you read there?' 27He replied, 'You must love the Lord your God with all your heart, with all your soul, with all your strength, and with all your mind, and your neighbour as yourself.' 28'You have answered right,' said Jesus, 'do this and life is yours.' 29But the man was anxious to justify himself, and said to Jesus, 'And who is my neighbour?' 30Jesus replied, 'A man was once on his way down from Jerusalem to Jericho and fell into the hands of brigands; they took all he had, beat him and then made off, leaving him half dead. 31Now a priest happened to be traveling down the same road, but when he saw the man, he passed by on the other side. 32In the same way, a Levite who came to the place saw him, and passed by on the other side. 33But a Samaritan traveller who came upon him was moved with compassion when he saw him. 34He went up and bandaged his wounds, pouring oil and wine on them. He then lifted him on to his own mount, carried him to the inn and looked after him. 35Next day, he took out two denarii and handed them to the innkeeper. "Look after him," he said "and on my way back I will make good any extra expense you have." 36Which of these three, do you think, proved himself a neighbour to the man who fell into the brigands' hands?' 37'The one who took pity on him' he replied. Jesus said to him, 'Go and do the same yourself.'

The gospel text for the Sunday is taken mainly with the parable of the Good Samaritan, one of the most famous of all of Jesus' parables.

A familiar text like this one poses problems for meditation, however – we know it so well that we tend to take for granted what it will be saying to us. You must make an effort to come to it as if for the first time.

As with all parables, enter into the movement until you recognise the specific moment which you can identify with, and then allow that moment to reveal something to you about life, about your relationship with God, and the work of his grace.

It is a complex story, with many themes woven into it. There

is the fact that a Samaritan is involved; the contrast between him
and the priest and Levite (vs. 31 and 32); the double aspect of his
response – compassion on the one hand (vs. 33) and very practical steps on the other (vs. 34 and 35).

Understand where the priest and the Levite were coming
from. According to Jewish law, touching a dead body made a
person unclean (Num 19:11-13). If the man happened to be dead,
the priest and the Levite, who were on their way to the temple in
Jerusalem, could not have officiated at the temple; therefore they
could not take the risk of helping the man.

The parable is set within a dialogue between Jesus and a
lawyer (vs. 25 to 29, and 36 to 37). Feel free to focus on this dialogue, identifying with Jesus, the ideal spiritual guide, or with
the lawyer, symbol of all of us when we come to God (or to people) seeking to justify ourselves.

* * *

Lord, often in our prayer we ask you questions,
but deep down we want to justify ourselves
– our inertia, our self-righteousness,
our secret racism or snobbishness.
We thank you that you continue to be Jesus for us,
entering into dialogue with us,
letting us come to our own conclusions,
occasionally giving us a push by saying,
'Go and do the same thing yourself.'

Lord, forgive us that as a church
we remain wrapped up in our concerns,
    - changes in the liturgy,
    - which are the most powerful prayers,
    - who should be bishops,
    - where parish boundaries should be set,
when all the while, down the same road we are walking,
people have fallen into the hands of brigands
who have left them half-dead.

'Love is a resurrection person scooping up the dust and chanting "live!"' Emily Dickinson

Lord, we remember with gratitude
a time in our lives when we felt beaten up,
half-dead at the side of the road.
Several people travelled down the same road and saw us
but passed by on the other side.
We thank you, Lord, for that person who came upon us,
saw us and was moved with compassion.
The person was a Samaritan
but somehow that did not seem to matter.
All we knew was that our wounds were being bandaged
and oil and wine poured on them,
that we were being lifted up and carried to an inn,
were being looked after and no one was being inconvenienced.
Lord, thank you for that good Samaritan;
help us to do the same for others ourselves.

'We can get along, we've got to; let's try to work it out.' Rodney King,
during the Los Angeles riots, May 1992

Lord, we remember societies torn apart
on the grounds of race, religion, culture or class
– Northern Ireland, the Middle East, Sudan,
the ghettos of North America and Europe.
We thank you that in all these communities
there are Samaritans,
quite unconcerned whether someone is a Jew or not,
just moved with compassion for a brother or sister
beaten and lying half-dead at the side of the road.
We pray that those who hear their stories
will go and do the same themselves.

'I go to church and just relax with my God. I relax and gather my strength in the Lord.' Emma Mashinimi, South African trade unionist,
January 1992

Lord, prayer is feeling well and truly beaten
and lying half-dead on the side of the road,
seeing church officials passing by on the other side,
then suddenly experiencing

that you yourself are moved with compassion for us,
that our wounds are being bandaged,
and oil and wine are being poured on them,
and knowing that we will be looked after
not merely now but for the future.

'Your cloister must be the streets of the city and your chapel the parish church.' St Vincent de Paul, founder of the first active order of religious
Lord, we thank you for the many religious
who serve you by travelling the roads
so that they come upon those lying on the side of the road,
bandage their wounds and pour oil and wine on them,
and inspire others to go and do the same themselves.

'We let ideas contend, but there must ultimately be an end to contention; there comes a time for decisions.' West Indian Commission, Report on West Indian Unity, June 1992
Lord, our leaders spend time asking theoretical questions,
often because they are anxious to justify themselves.
Send us people who will tell them
about the Samaritans in our society
who care for those who have been beaten up
and are lying half-dead on our roads,
and then challenge them to go and do the same themselves.

Sixteenth Sunday in Ordinary Time

Gospel reading: Luke 10:38-42

38*Jesus came to a village, and a woman named Martha welcomed him into her house.* 39*She had a sister called Mary, who sat down at the Lord's feet and listened to him speaking.* 40*Now Martha who was distracted with all the serving said, 'Lord, do you not care that my sister is leaving me to do the serving all by myself? Please tell her to help me.'* 41*But the Lord answered, 'Martha, Martha,' he said 'you worry and fret about so many things,* 42*and yet few are needed, indeed only one. It is Mary who has chosen the better part; it is not to be taken from her.'*

Here is another very famous story which you must meditate on personally, letting yourself be guided by your feelings.

The passage has given rise to deep and sometimes mystical interpretations, but at root it is a simple story of human relationships and your meditation must start there.

You may like to focus on Jesus. See him as a model human being, receiving the hospitality of the sisters, accepting the love of Mary, teaching Martha wisdom, kindly but firmly.

Though the Catholic tradition has tended to favour Mary over Martha, some have found that Martha was in fact the more mature of the two. Identify with whichever of the two you feel attracted to, letting the other one be a lesson by way of contrast.

The key to the passage is the little phrase 'the better part'. Your personal meditation will guide you in making your interpretation.

* * *

Lord, many people misunderstand hospitality.
They worry and fret
about preparing plenty of food and decorating the house.
But few things are needed to make people feel at home,
indeed only one, which is to sit with our guests
and listen to them speaking.

Lord, we pray for parents today.
Let them not fall into the error of worrying and fretting

about doing many things for their children,
then complaining that no one is helping them.
Remind them that the only essential thing
is to sit down at the feet of their children and listen to them.

Lord, so often we keep busy,
complaining about all we have to do,
and that our brothers and sisters
are leaving us to do all the work by ourselves.
We even ask you to tell them to help us.
We thank you for that day
when you sent someone to speak to us
    - a sermon in church,
    - one of our children told us we were insincere,
    - we found ourselves committing a sin.
We felt hurt and angry.
But now we realise that it was Jesus speaking to us
as he spoke to Martha,
showing us that we really were running away
from the one thing we needed more than any other,
to spend more time at prayer,
to sit at your feet and listen
as you show us the truth about ourselves.

'The creator, the source of all, is in the heart of each one of us.'
The Upanishads
Lord, there is a Martha and a Mary within each of us
    - a part of ourselves which is active and busy,
    - another part which sits at your feet and listens trustingly to
      your word.
We need our active self to accomplish your will,
but the listening self is the best part,
and we must not allow it to be taken from us.

Lord, we thank you for listening communities,
    -Bible sharing groups;
    - alcoholics anonymous;
    - Montessori schools.
What marks them out from others is simplicity.

Those responsible know
that few things are needed to make a community,
and the one thing that must not be taken away
is listening to every member of the group
as if sitting at the Lord's feet.

*'The West Indian people have not waited on governments; they have
integrated in their own informal but highly effective way.'* Report of the
West Indian Commission, June 1992

Lord, we pray for our leaders.
They worry and fret about many things, and even complain
that the people leave them to do the serving all by themselves,
when in fact they are neglecting the one thing
that is needed most of all,
which is to sit at the feet of their people and listen to them.

Seventeenth Sunday in Ordinary Time

Gospel reading: Luke 11:1-13

1Once Jesus was in a certain place praying, and when he had finished one of his disciples said, 'Lord, teach us to pray, just as John taught his disciples.' 2He said to them, 'Say this when you pray: Father, may your name be held holy, your kingdom come; 3give us each day our daily bread, and forgive us our sins, 4for we ourselves forgive each one who is in debt to us. And do not put us to the test.' 5He also said to them, 'Suppose one of you has a friend and goes to him in the middle of the night to say, "My friend, lend me three loaves, 6because a friend of mine on his travels has just arrived at my house and I have nothing to offer him"; 7and the man answers from inside the house, "Do not bother me. The door is bolted now, and my children and I are in bed; I cannot get up to give it you." 8I tell you, if the man does not get up and give it him for friendship's sake, persistence will be enough to make him get up and give his friends all he wants. 9I say to you: Ask, and it will be given to you; search, and you will find; knock, and the door will be opened to you. 10For the one who asks always receives; the one who searches always finds; the one who knocks will always have the door opened to him. 11What father among you would hand his son a stone when he asked for bread? Or hand him a snake instead of a fish? 12Or hand him a scorpion if he asked for an egg? 13If you then, who are evil, know how to give your children what is good, how much more will the heavenly Father give the Holy Spirit to those who ask him!'

Jesus' teaching on prayer in this passage has many aspects. There is no need to look for an overall logic in the passage; just choose the aspect that touches you here and now.

Verse 1: the disciples ask Jesus to teach them how to pray.

Verses 2-4: the Lord's prayer. As the introductory words indicate, the prayer was given not so much as a formula, but as a style of prayer. The following verses will help you identify what this style is.

The prayer is Luke's version, which is slightly different from the one we are accustomed to which comes mostly from Matthew 5:9-13.

Verses 5-8: this is a parable. As in last week's meditation, discover what is for you the significant moment of the story; it will lead you to the word God has for you in this parable.

In verses 9 to 13, the parable is interpreted by Jesus, although as a teaching it can stand on its own. To get the full teaching in verses 9 and 10, you must take literally the word 'always' repeated three times. There is a tendency to water it down, and as a result the message is lost.

Enter into the movement of verses 11 and 13, and the dramatic style of the teaching.

* * *

'The modern world listens more willingly to witnesses than to teachers, and if it does listen to teachers, it is because they are witnesses.'
Pope Paul VI, *Evangelii Nuntiandi*

Lord, remind us
that the most effective way to teach others how to pray,
is for them to find us praying,
and when we are finished to ask us to teach them how we do it.

Lord, many people today
are learning to pray in traditions that are foreign to us
– TM, yoga, Zen meditation.
We pray that, as Jesus did for his disciples,
his church may hear the cry of its members
asking to be taught how to pray.

'In this world monopoly, do we ever 'pass go' or do we 'go straight to jail'?' David Rudder, Trinidad calypsonian

Lord, we thank you for moments of prayer
when we find within ourselves a hope
that your name will be held holy and your kingdom come.

*'When I give bread to the hungry, they call me a saint; when I ask why the hungry have no bread, they call me a commun*ist.' Helder Camara

Lord, help us, when we pray for the coming of your kingdom,
to ask for it in its entirety.
Keep us searching for the day
when every one will have each day their daily bread,
when those in debt will be freed of all their indebtedness,
and poor people will no longer be put to the test of survival.

*'We should let ourselves be brought naked and defenceless before God,
without explanation, without theories, completely dependent upon his
providential care, in dire need of the gift of his grace, his mercy and the
light of faith.'* Thomas Merton

Lord, you have revealed yourself to us as friend,
and that has been helpful.
But it could lead us to become complacent,
as if you owe us favours.
So every once in a while we experience you
as someone who gives us our daily bread
not from friendship but because we persist
in knocking at your door.
Thank you, Lord.

'Prayer is the union of nothing with the Nothing.' Augustine Baker,
English mystic

Lord, forgive us that we have made prayer into a bargain,
where in exchange for our asking we receive your favours.
Bring us to that prayer which is merely knocking at a door
that is already open,
searching in the dark for something that is already found.

Lord, we sometimes think
we have to leave our experience to get close to you.
But Jesus taught us to start with what we have known.
So today, we thank you for those who love us,
friends, parents, spiritual guides, teachers,
the kind of people we know if ever we asked them for bread,
no way would they give us a stone,
or if we asked them for fish, no way would they hand us a snake,
and if we asked them for an egg,
no way would they hand us a scorpion.
Lord, these people are good
but their goodness cannot compare with yours.

Eighteenth Sunday in Ordinary Time

13*A man in the crowd said to Jesus, 'Master, tell my brother to give me a share of our inheritance.'* 14*'My friend,' he replied, 'who appointed me your judge, or the arbitrator of your claims?'* 15*Then he said to them, 'Watch, and be on your guard against avarice of any kind, for a man's life is not made secure by what he owns, even when he has more then he needs.'* 16*Then he told them a parable: 'There was once a rich man who, having had a good harvest from the land,* 17*thought to himself, 'What am I to do? I have not enough room to store my crops.'* 18*Then he said, 'This is what I will do: I will pull down my barns and build bigger ones, and store all my grain and my goods in them,* 19*and I will say to my soul: My soul, you have plenty of good things laid by for many years to come; take things easy, eat, drink, have a good time.'* 20*But God said to him, 'Fool! This very night the demand will be made for your soul; and this hoard of yours, whose will it be then?'* 21*So it is when a man stores up treasure for himself in place of making himself rich in the sight of God.'*

The passage is in several sections:
- verses 13 and 14: a dialogue between Jesus and the man;
- verse 15: a teaching on avarice;.
- verses 16 to 21: a parable with its explanation.

If you decide to meditate on the dialogue, you can identify with Jesus, the leader who refuses to play games with people, or the man, whom we will recognise as ourselves when we pray (or relate with people) from self-interest.

The teaching on avarice is imaginative, as Jesus' teachings always are. You might like to ask yourself who has been Jesus in your life.

The parable has two moments, each of which can unveil reality to you. There is the moment when the man decided to build bigger barns, and the one when God called him. This second moment has two aspects: his soul was demanded of him, and he had to face the question, 'This hoard of yours, whose will it be?'

The brief interpretation in verse 21 seems simple at first reading, but personal meditation can reveal how deep it really is.

Lord, forgive us for the times when we make prayer
an occasion for getting you to tell our brothers
to give us a share of our inheritance,
as if you were some kind of high court judge
or arbitrator of our claims.

*'The ultimate purpose of trade and industry is to serve our fellow
human beings by creating goods and services to meet their needs.'*
George Carey, Archbishop of Canterbury
Lord, we pray that your church may always be
the voice of Jesus in our modern world,
challenging our contemporaries to watch and be on their guard
against avarice of any kind,
and reminding them that our lives are not made secure
by what we own,
even when we have more than we need.

*'Materialism has failed as an ideology in the East, but it has certainly
triumphed as a matter of practice in the West.'* President Havel of
 Czechoslovakia
Lord, we thank you for those few world leaders
who are the voice of Jesus in our day,
calling us to watch and be on our guard
against avarice of every kind.

*'The continued greed of the wealthy nations will certainly call down on
them the wrath of the poor, with consequences no one can foretell.'* Pope
Paul VI, *Populorum Progressio*
Lord, the wealthy nations of the world
have had good harvests from their land,
they have pulled down their barns and built bigger ones,
storing their grain and their goods in them.
They think that they have plenty of good things laid by
for many years to come
and so they can take things easy, drink and have a good time.
But the time will surely come
when the poor nations of the world
will demand to be treated as members of the human family,
and that great hoard of goods, whose will it be then?

'The Cross is the power of truth. It exposes the ultimate futility of relationships based on fear, manipulation and violence.'
Bishop Raymond Hunthausen of Seattle

Lord, we remember a time
when something terrible happened to us
- a death in the family;
- we were humiliated in front of our friends;
- we discovered how jealous we were.
Truly our souls were being demanded of us.
We realised then that we are not made secure by what we own,
that the treasures we store up for ourselves are really worthless.
We thank you that at that moment
we felt poor and very vulnerable,
but also very rich because we knew
that you looked on us with love.

'Hell is not to love any more.' Dorothy Day

Lord, the worst experience in the whole world
is to have a demand made for our souls
and then to realise
that we have stored up treasures for ourselves
in place of making ourselves rich in your sight.

'By admitting death into our lives we enlarge and enrich them.'
Etty Hillesum, Jewish woman who died in a concentration camp, 1943

Lord, remind us always
of that dread moment when you will say to us:
'This very night demand will be made of your soul.'
When our horizons are not limited by the big barns
in which we have stored our grain and all our goods,
we can become truly rich.

'We cannot allow the politicians to cloud our vision and promote their disruptive policies, as it would lead to our destruction.'
Lloyd Best, Trinidad economist

Lord, help us to stand up to leaders
whose main interest is building big barns
in which to store all their grain and goods,
thinking they have plenty of good things laid by

for many years to come,
when all the time they are destroying the tolerance
that has made us a wealthy nation in your sight.

Nineteenth Sunday in Ordinary Time

Gospel reading: Luke 12:35-40

35*Jesus said to his disciples: 'See that you are dressed for action and have your lamps lit.* 36*Be like men waiting for their master to return from the wedding feast, ready to open the door as soon as he comes and knocks.* 37*Happy those servants whom the master finds awake when he comes. I tell you solemnly, he will put on an apron, sit them down at table and wait on them.* 38*It may be in the second watch he comes, or in the third, but happy those servants if he finds them ready.* 39*You may be quite sure of this, that if the householder had known at what hour the burglar would come, he would not have let anyone break through the wall of his house.* 40*You too must stand ready, because the Son of Man is coming at an hour you do not expect.'*

The gospel passage for this Sunday consists of sayings of Jesus, so it would be good to look first at some general principles that must be respected in interpreting sayings.

Remember, first, that in gospel meditation a passage must be read very slowly. I mention this because the sayings of Jesus are short, and often people tend to read them quickly. This happens especially in a passage like this, where we have several sayings on one general theme. It is, however, not a logically constructed teaching, but a collection of sayings, each one different and with its own way of putting across the theme. We must therefore take them separately, letting each one in turn rest in our hearts. Each one is like a special wine, and God invites us to be connoisseurs who take time to savour each one and discover its distinctive flavour.

Secondly, the sayings of Jesus are usually metaphors, speaking to our imagination. This is another point that we are inclined to forget, because in the modern Western world teachers speak in the abstract and to the reason. We must make an effort to stir up our feelings, bringing back memories of our own deep experience, or the experience of people who have touched our lives. In this way we discover for ourselves the truth of the sayings, and within this process we experience God calling us to spiritual growth. This will take time, especially when – as we shall see in some of the sayings in this passage – the metaphor is complex and leads us in more than one direction.

Finally, the sayings of Jesus are universally true. Many people read them as true only of our relationship with God, and of spiritual growth. But they also apply to what happens to our church communities, our village, our country, and the world. We must be open to discovering this universality, so that gradually (it always takes time) we enter into the many ways in which the saying is true.

The Metaphor of Waiting

All the sayings in this passage are about waiting. This is a difficult metaphor for us today, because in our culture we experience waiting as something negative. 'I am waiting' means that I am doing nothing and furthermore that I resent it: 'How could you keep me waiting?'

For the Bible, however – and this is good common sense – waiting is a creative moment, or at least can be if we enter freely into it. When I wait for others, I give them the space to be themselves, paying them the respect of letting them exercise their creativity, and I do it not with indifference or grudgingly, but with love, so that we can walk together in solidarity and mutual enrichment.

It is in this perspective that we must understand the Bible expression 'waiting for God', which we find, for example, in Psalm 146:

'His delight is not in horses
nor his pleasure in warrior strength.
The Lord delights in those who revere him,
in those who wait for his love.'

People sometimes imagine God sitting in heaven and looking down at his creatures. God in the Bible is not like this at all. 'My Father goes on working,' St John quotes Jesus saying, 'and so do I.' God is always at work in our lives, in the lives of others and in the world, and this work is always to break the rod of the oppressor and to set captives free.

To wait for God is, then, to say to him that we know he is at work, and we are prepared to let him carry out his loving purpose when and how he pleases. At times, of course, we become impatient, and even panic and cry out, 'How long, O Lord!' But at other times, we feel able to make our act of adoration and tell God that we are willing to wait for him.

The moment is also creative for ourselves. When we wait, our latent tendencies to dominate and manipulate come to the surface, so that we are open to experiencing this as a moment of grace – we will go beyond these evil tendencies and enter that deep inner space where we are in trusting communion with God and with one another; free in ourselves and allowing others to be free.

As you read this passage, then, and enter into the various sayings, remember waiting experiences that were moments of grace for you or for others. The times when you were able to wait for a child or a friend, and, at some unexpected moment, they opened up to you and you entered into a new and deeper relationship with them. Perhaps you struggled for years with drinking or drugs or an unhealthy relationship; you went through agony, unable to make up your mind about moving into a new lifestyle; and then one day the way became perfectly clear and easy; reading this passage today, you realise what it means to wait for God's moment. Be with people you know who are tired of waiting; read the passage in solidarity with them, letting the message flow through you so that it touches them and renews their courage.

Waiting is important in our relationship with a community too, a church community or any other. So often we try to manipulate a community rather than letting it grow organically according to its own dynamic. As you read this passage, remember great leaders you have known who have trusted the community, knew how to wait for it, according to the saying that everything happens in its own time; and so, when the moment came, the growth was solid, 'the seed grew tall and strong,' as Jesus expressed it in the Parable of the Sower.

This teaching on waiting is tremendously important today, when influencing people has become a skill that can be acquired like any other; when people boast openly that given sufficient money, they can make the public buy anything, not excluding a President or Prime Minister at election time. In this cultural context, we Christians will be tempted to think that grace can also be manipulated in this way, and that if only we could buy more time on television, or if our religious magazines were more glossy, or if we could work more sensational miracles, people would be converted. These sayings remind us that the laws of spiritual growth are different, and we remember with gratitude that in this area earthly power achieves little, but there is real power in trust, care and compassion – all that is implied in waiting.

Our age needs this teaching for another reason too. The church communities of the New Testament time had little social or political influence. We tend to forget this, because the Roman Emperor became a Christian and, before long, Christianity became the official religion of the State. In the early years, however, there was no prospect whatsoever that this would ever happen. We can see why, in such a context, there was so much emphasis on a self-confident faith which would enable Christians to look calmly at the great Roman Empire and still believe that the values of Jesus Christ would triumph in the end.

The metaphor of waiting expressed perfectly this kind of faith. Can we not say that this is precisely the faith we need today – a trust in the power of our values that takes away any great need for success or quick results?

Remembering the importance of this teaching, let us now turn to the collection of sayings.

Verse 35. A friend has told you that he will take you out for a pint, but it is now very late and he hasn't turned up. Your parents, all your brothers and sisters have gone to bed, and you are still there, dressed to go out, and the lights in the house are still on. Your mother puts her head out of her room, 'You still waiting? Why don't you go to bed?' You shake your head stubbornly, 'I know he will come.' Jesus is telling us that faith in him is like that; everybody else has sold out to the prevailing value system, they have fallen asleep, as it is often expressed in the New Testament, but you continue to believe that the values of Jesus will come good. We think with gratitude of Martin Luther King saying, as he received the Noble Peace Prize, 'I still believe that unarmed truth and unconditional love will have the final word in reality.'

Note that the saying is in the form of a command – 'see that...'

– which can be interpreted in two ways. It can be read as a warning – 'better be careful or you will fall away like everyone else.' But it can also be a word of encouragement – 'Don't worry about all the negative signs you see all around you; I can promise you that I am coming soon.' Either way, we see here the role of the church or of the individual Christian to be the voice of Jesus in the World today.

Verse 36 points us in a new direction. We are waiting for a master who is away at a wedding feast. We Christians live in the real world with all its selfishness and its fragmentation; but we know that our master is celebrating a world of harmony and reconciliation, and the vision of that world gives direction and hope to our lives.

The verse also evokes for us the moment of grace always coming suddenly, as we saw above; and we respond immediately or not at all:

'There is a tide in the affairs of men,
which taken at the flood leads on to fortune;
omitted, all the voyage of their life
is bound in shallows and miseries.'

Remember the times when God knocked, fresh from the celebration of harmony, and somehow or other you were able to open immediately; you were able to give up that bad habit, to forgive, to move into a new and deeper relationship. Pray for those you know who are struggling that they may continue to wait in trust, ready to open the door as soon as the Lord comes and knocks.

Verse 37 focuses on the blessedness that comes over us when we have waited long and eventually experienced the moment of grace. It is as if a great and generous master whom we admire greatly, has put on an apron, has sat us down at table and is attending to our every need. We feel perfectly secure, all our anxieties have vanished, and we know that it has not been our achievement – he who is mighty has done great things to his servant.

Verse 38 reminds us that waiting always seems long, just as the hours of the night seem longer than we had bargained for. You thought it would be for the first watch, but it isn't; it must surely be the second then, but it isn't; and you realise that it mightn't be the third either. Is not the fulfilment of our deepest aspirations like that? Who was the Jesus that God sent into your life to encourage you to continue waiting?

In verse 39 the metaphor shifts again. It is the moment when a person recognises humbly, 'he fooled me again' – the boxer became careless and let his guard drop; defenders were over-confident and let the forwards come through to score. I thought I was beyond lust and jealousy; our community was acting as if ambition, racism or snobbishness were dead among us; now we look ruefully at the wall of our house in a shambles and we reflect that if we had known at what hour the burglar would come we would not have let anyone break through it. We should not read this verse with bitterness, nor should we understand it to say that we must spend our whole lives on guard. God is inviting us to laugh at ourselves, caught out once again, and we know that a humble and contrite heart is worth more than tens of thousands of fatted lambs offered in sacrifice.

The 'Son of Man' in verse 40 is a messianic term, the Saviour, the great leader whom God sends to rescue the oppressed. This verse is therefore a call to renewed hope. It is Isaiah and John the Baptist and all the prophets proclaiming to those who feel lost and abandoned not to lose heart because just at the moment when they feel most lost, the moment when they least expect it, God will intervene to save them. Remember when you experienced the truth of this saying, the times when you were just about to despair and against all the odds, the Son of Man came. Now say this to others: 'You too must stand ready.'

* * *

Lord, we thank you for the times you said to us
that it is not enough for us to be ready to go somewhere,
dressed for action and with our lamps lit.
We must be like those who wait for their master
to return from the wedding feast,
ready to open the door as soon as he comes and knocks.
We must be quite sure that
happy are those once he finds them ready.
We too must always stand ready because the Son of Man
will be coming at an hour we do not expect.

The Assumption

Gospel reading: Luke 1:39-56

[39]*Mary set out at that time and went as quickly as she could to a town in the hill country of Judah.* [40]*She went into Zachariah's house and greeted Elizabeth.* [41]*Now as soon as Elizabeth heard Mary's greeting, the child leapt in the womb and Elizabeth was filled with the Holy Spirit.* [42]*She gave a loud cry and said, 'Of all women you are the most blessed, and blessed is the fruit of your womb.* [43]*Why should I be honoured with a visit from the mother of my Lord?* [44]*For the moment your greeting reached my ears, the child in my womb leapt for joy.* [45]*Yes, blessed is she who believed that the promise made her by the Lord would be fulfilled.'*

[46]*And Mary said; 'My soul proclaims the greatness of the Lord*
[47]*and my spirit exults in God my saviour,*

[48]*because he has looked upon his lowly handmaid. Yes, from this day forward all generations will call me blessed,* [49]*for the Almighty has done great things for me. Holy is his name,* [50]*and his mercy reaches from age to age for those who fear him.*

[51]*He has shown the power of his arm, he has routed the proud of heart.*

[52]*He has pulled down princes from their thrones and exalted the lowly.*

[53]*The hungry he has filled with good things, the rich sent away empty.*

[54]*He has come to the help of Israel his servant, mindful of his mercy*
[55]*– according to the promise he made to our ancestors –*

[56]*of his mercy to Abraham and to his descendants for ever.'*

Today's gospel passage is in two sections. They were composed separately and are different in character:
    - verses 39 to 45 and 56 are narrative, the story of the visitation of Mary to Elizabeth;
    - verses 46 to 55 are a prayer.
It is difficult to meditate on both sections at one time; today I am proposing a meditation on the Magnificat.

The Magnificat is Mary's personal prayer, made on the specific occasion of her meeting with Elizabeth; but it is also a universal prayer, as Christians have recognised through the centuries – one of the best loved of Christian prayers. When we meditate on the Magnificat, we identify with Mary as she 'stands out among the poor and humble of the Lord who confidently hope for and receive salvation from him' (Second Vatican Council, Document on the Church).

The Magnificat is primarily a prayer of thanksgiving, but as with all biblical prayers, once we enter into it we will find ourselves moving spontaneously into other aspects of our relationship with God. With Mary we thank God for his grace, but the words of the prayer lead us to ask for a fuller outpouring of his grace and even its final fulfilment. The prayer also reminds us of how we fall short of what God wants us to be, so that it becomes a call to conversion.

Our meditation will lead us into the many dimensions of the Magnificat. It is a personal prayer but also the prayer of the church and indeed of all humanity. We celebrate (and long for) our individual victories of grace but also the social victories, the righting of injustices in communities – families, church, country and world.

With a well-known text such as this one, we must make a special effort to be concrete in our meditation. We must ask ourselves in whose name we are praying the Magnificat: our family? A particular individual? Our church community? Humanity?

We must also concretise the images: in what way has God 'looked upon' us (or our communities)? What are the 'great things' he has done for us? How has he 'shown the power of his arm'? Who are the 'princes' he has 'pulled down from their thrones'? In what sense has he 'filled the hungry with good things'?

We must be careful to interpret verses 50 and 52 in the light of the constant New Testament teaching that we 'love those who persecute us'. If we find ourselves gloating over 'princes' being 'pulled down from their thrones' or 'the rich being sent away empty' our meditation has taken a wrong turning. We can avoid that error in one of two ways. We identify the 'proud of heart', the 'princes', not with individuals, but with forces within ourselves or in society – arrogance, elitism, a sense of inferiority, racism, sexism, and so on. Or we take 'routing', 'pulling down' and 'sending away empty' as a moment of grace when oppressors of the poor (including ourselves) are brought to repent of their evil ways.

Lord, as we contemplate Mary,
the lowly virgin of Nazareth now assumed in heaven,
we celebrate all the lowly people of the world
who are lifted up before our eyes.
We think of those who face difficult situations with courage,
do not let themselves be overwhelmed
by the evils they experience,
find time and energy to celebrate the gifts you have given them,
are nourished by the faith that
whatever life has in store for them,
they are safe in your hands.
We celebrate in particular
- parents who continue to care for their children when they
  are on drugs, in irregular relationships, embarked on a life of
  crime;
- men and women whose spouses were unfaithful and who
  accept them back in sickness or old age;
- leaders of communities torn apart by conflict who persevere in working for reconciliation and end up being attacked
  by all the parties involved;
- individuals battling with their weaknesses, addiction, depression, lack of self-confidence, jealousy;
- the terminally ill and those who have contracted AIDS.
Lord, we thank you in the name of all these Marys,
those of today and those of the past,
we proclaim your greatness,
and our spirits exult in you, our Saviour.

There are times when we feel discouraged
- disappointed by someone we considered a friend,
- looked down upon by those who are more successful than
  we are,
- mocked by those who say, 'I told you so!'
- ashamed within our own selves.
But we hold our heads high because we know
that even if we are lowly in the eyes of others
you send us Elizabeth who looks upon us with love and respect.
The future may look bleak,
but we remember that from this day forward

all generations will call us blessed.
We have been failures in the eyes of some,
but you have done great things for us,
and holy is your name,
your mercy reaches from age to age to those who fear you.
When we feel powerless before the obstacles in our path
– many of them within our own selves,
others put there by people,
including some who think they are acting for our good –
help us to remember the power of your arm,
how you will rout all the forces
that oppose your loving plan for us.
They seem too great for us now,
but you will pull them down from their thrones and exalt us;
they are like wild beasts ready to devour us,
but you will fill us with good things
and send them away empty handed.

Lord, we thank you that you look on us
as the Israel of our time, your servants,
and that you come to our help,
mindful of your unconditional love,
according to the covenant you made with our ancestors
that you would never go back on the love
you promised to Abraham and his descendants for ever.

Lord, we pray that our church communities
will be your dwelling place on earth
where the lowly ones of the world
– the poor, the aged and the children, those who are shunned by
the wider society, strangers, immigrants, refugees, minorities
from different religious or ethnic groups –
are welcomed; where they will exult
because they are called blessed,
and the great things you have done for them are celebrated;
where the proud of heart are routed,
those who set themselves up as princes over others
are pulled down from their thrones and the lowly are exalted,
the hungry are so filled with good things

that those of us who thought we were rich
now realise that we have been sent away empty.
We pray that your church, the true Israel your servant,
will always remember your preferential love for the poor
and the promises you made to Abraham
and his descendants for ever are fulfilled.

Lord, help us to keep alive
the dream of your kingdom as Mary saw it,
a world where there is no lording over others,
where princes are pulled down from their thrones
and the lowly are lifted up,
the hungry are filled with good things
and the rich walk humbly alongside them,
where all receive the good things of the world
as expressions of your merciful love,
the fulfilment of your promises
to Abraham and his descendants for ever.

Twentieth Sunday in Ordinary Time

Gospel reading: Luke 12:49-53

49*Jesus said to his disciples: 'I have come to bring fire to the earth, and how I wish it were blazing already!* 50*There is a baptism I must still receive, and how great is my distress till it is over!* 51*Do you suppose that I am here to bring peace on earth? No, I tell you, but rather division.* 52*For from now on a household of five will be divided: three against two and two against three;* 53*the father divided against the son, son against father, mother against daughter, daughter against mother, mother-in-law against daughter-in-law, daughter-in-law against mother-in-law.'*

The gospel passage for this Sunday is in three sections
- verse 49;
- verse 50;
- and verses 51 to 53.

As I have often recommended, you should meditate on one section at a time. But you will find that in this passage the three sections complement one another; if taken together, they correct any false interpretations which could arise if they were read separately. Think of them, therefore, as parts of a beautifully constructed building in which each part is appreciated in relation to the whole.

The metaphor of fire in verse 49 is difficult to tie down, because it is a common one and can be interpreted in many different ways. In fact, it is used with a variety of interpretations in the Bible itself: the tongues of fire representing the coming of the Spirit; the burning fire of love, and so on. The interpretation probably intended by Jesus in this passage is the one we find in chapter 3 of St Luke's gospel, where John the Baptist said that the Messiah would come and baptise with the Holy Spirit and with fire, and went on to explain that he would gather God's pure wheat into the barn and dispatch the chaff to be burnt in a fire that would never go out. In our passage, then, Jesus is at a moment in his life – one that we can identify with – when he is deeply moved by all the chaff in the world, the phoniness, the arrogance, the oppression, and he longs to see it going up in a great bonfire, while true goodness is gathered safely into God's barn.

Secondly, the sayings of Jesus are usually metaphors, speaking to our imagination. You say the words with Jesus, then, getting in touch with the particular form of chaff that makes you indignant – hypocrisy, or racism, or manipulation – and getting in touch with the particular part of 'the earth' where you see it – your family, your church community, your country or some other country, your own self. Experience with Jesus the blessedness of hungering and thirsting for God's justice to be realised in the world.

Thank God for those people you have known who saw it as their mission in life ('I have come to...') to expose evil in one of its hidden forms and refuse to accept it passively as we are inclined to do. Put their names into the verse so that you can experience that the Spirit of Jesus is still in the world.

There is a danger that we will read verse 49 self-righteously or fanatically, and it has often been read like this, Christians covering up a natural hardness or intolerance with the pretence that it was the will of God.

Verse 50 comes, therefore, as a corrective. Jesus is anxious to cast fire, but he took no pleasure in this; he expressed his feelings with the metaphor of a baptism with which he had to be baptised, not referring to the sacrament, but using the word in its original sense of drowning. He felt he was being thrown into a dark abyss and he was afraid. Identify with him at this moment. All his life has been leading here, he knew it was the only way to go, that he would be bringing new life for the world, and yet, he was afraid. This was the moment the synoptic gospels recorded as the agony in the garden and St John in Chapter 12 verse 27:

'Now my soul is troubled.
And what should I say –
"Father, save me from this hour."?
No, it is for this reason that I have come to this hour.
Father, glorify your name.'

The Epistle to the Hebrews also describes this moment: 'He offered up prayer and entreaty, aloud and in silent tears to the one who had power to save him out of death.' The prophet Hababuk had the same feeling as he waited for a moment of grace:

'My whole body trembles,
my lips quiver at the sound;
decay creeps into my bones,
my steps falter beneath me.'

Be with people who are living that moment, knowing that they are doing the right thing and yet insecure and afraid of the hurts they will cause others, 'carrying with them in their bodies the death of Jesus,' as St Paul described it.

Finally, enter into the movement of verses 51-53, with its 'do you suppose?' and 'no'. Remember a time when you took for granted that the teaching of Jesus was going to make life easier for you, and someone or some event brought you up short, hitting you with the realisation, 'Hey! It isn't like that at all.' That was Jesus entering your life.

Respond to the concreteness of the teaching. It is a family of five: mother, father, a married son with his wife and a daughter, and they are divided three against two and two against three. Let the repetitiveness touch you so that you experience the continued pain and the frustration of the division. Then bring Jesus into the story, looking on at that painful situation and saying that it is what has to be. See him as the great leader, not hiding the facts, nor abdicating his responsibility, and thank God for people you have known who were like that.

* * *

Lord, we thank you
that you know there is a fire you want to bring to the earth
and you wish it were blazing already.
We know that you did not come to bring peace on earth
but rather division.
We thank you for the times
when you brought some separation between us
and people we knew were very close to us.

Twenty-First Sunday in Ordinary Time

Gospel reading: Luke 13:22-30

22Through towns and villages he went teaching, making his way to Jerusalem. 23Someone said to him, 'Sir, will there be only a few saved?' He said to them, 24'Try your best to enter by the narrow door, because, I tell you, many will try to enter and will not succeed. 25Once the master of the house has got up and locked the door, you may find yourself knocking on the door, saying, 'Lord, open to us' but he will answer, 'I do not know where you come from.' 26Then you will find yourself saying, 'We once ate and drank in your company; you taught in our streets,' 27but he will reply, 'I do not know where you come from. Away from me, all you wicked men!' 28Then there will be weeping and grinding of teeth, when you see Abraham and Isaac and Jacob and all the prophets in the kingdom of God, and yourself turned outside. 29And men from east and west, from north and south, will come to take their places at the feast in the kingdom of God. 30Yes, there are those now last who will be first, and those now first who will be last.'

We can divide the passage into several sections and we can take each of them as something to be meditated on separately. We can also take them all as the answer to one basic question – to conquer any issue in life, we must move to a deeper level of our being.

Verse 22 makes an important point: as Jesus went teaching through towns and villages he was making his way to Jerusalem. This reminds us of an important aspect of Jesus' work. At every moment of his teaching, Jesus had a goal. There was something very precious that he wanted to achieve for himself and for everyone else.

Many today have the sentiment that failure was a necessary part of Jesus' purpose for a real life for his followers. This was not the fact however. His individual teachings were quite different. He wanted us to succeed and to have a full life. He wanted us all to have a life of goodness; he planned for a healthy life for everyone, no matter our personal gifts.

He wanted the entire kingdom of Israel to follow his teachings. He did not want to have his plan rejected. For him, this was a sad ending that he must accept but he did not really want it for himself. It was something he had to take, as we all have to.

In order for us all to be close to him however, he himself must go through the deep sufferings of those who die in sad situations. He must face up to people's feelings of being abandoned by God. They must be accustomed to know that he hasn't let them down. They must, as Jesus learnt to say on the cross, know that he hasn't forgotten them.

Only then will he be able to have men and women on his side. We can all be alongside him in all he wants for us. We must not take him away from this final goal which we know is part of his kingdom. Once this is clear, everything else will fit in. We must interpret the rest of his teachings in the light of this fact. It is part of his desire that all should follow him.

As preachers of a gospel message we must know the place where we want to end up ourselves. This has a great value for us and it will certainly affect how we relate with others. It will affect how we look on them.

Verses 23 and 24: Jesus is asked a question. It is one we are always inclined to ask – how many will be saved?

Jesus responds by insisting on one important point. The people who succeed must make a real effort to do so. The door we try to enter is always 'narrow' and therefore is always difficult to enter. We must try hard and put our best step forward. We try and we are truly sad when we know that we are not really sure that we will eventually be victorious over the forces of evil that are within us all.

Verses 25 to 27 lay down another important law. Many of those who we now consider to be holy people will eventually be rejected from God's kingdom. They will come to the house they are looking for but find that the master has it well locked and will let the doors remain closed from us.

As can be expected, former followers like ourselves will then find themselves knocking frantically on the door. We will say things like, 'Lord open to us' or 'we here are your special friends' or again, ' we are sure that when you see us, you will respond'. We find ourselves saying, 'we once ate and drank in your company' and we tell the master, 'you taught in our streets'. The Lord will merely say, 'I do not know where you come from.' He will then speak to us in the language spoken of in psalm 6, verse 8, 'away from me all you wicked men and women'. He doesn't really know us. This is the sad but very important news.

This therefore requires another deep commitment to salvation from those who feel meritorious of the kingdom.

Verses 28 to 29 speak of a double vision. It is one that is full of meaning for us in the world today. The present people, those who belong to what are called in our modern language, 'God's true church', will find themselves doing something very clear. We will see ourselves with 'weeping and grinding of teeth' as we see Abraham, and Isaac and Jacob and all the prophets in the kingdom of God' and others we used to look down on not with them. We ourselves will meanwhile be 'turned outside'. We will be left far away from God's own kingdom.

On the other hand, we will see 'men and women' who come from far. They will come from 'east and west' and then 'from north and south' and yet they will be within the kingdom. As former outsiders they will now come to take their place at the feast. Meanwhile those who were considered 'first' now find themselves 'last' – far away from God's own kingdom.

Verse 30 draws an obvious conclusion from the entire passage. Those who are now considered 'last' in the kingdom of God will then be seen to be first. This will be truly important for us.

Unfortunately there is another truth we must be well aware of. Those who are now considered 'first' will then be seen to be the 'last'. They will end up furthest from the kingdom of God whereas others will be seen to be 'first'. We must be aware of this crucial distinction as we go through our lives.

This entire passage now certainly appears as warning us against a complacent acceptance of ourselves as close to the kingdom of God. This can be a real help against any form of self-righteousness.

* * *

'The ancient way of thinking concentrated itself on knowing oneself, interiorly from within.' Jawaharl Nehru

Lord, we thank you that
just as you made your way to Jerusalem,
you continued to go through towns and villages,
reminding people that they too
must aim for the kingdom of God.
We too must hand on our teaching from this standpoint,
in full acceptance of our weakness.

Lord, prevent us from becoming complacent
about our entering the kingdom of God.
Teach us to wait as we go on through life.
Tell us how to stand by with humility,
so that we can truly enter by a door that is very narrow.
We know that many will try to enter and will not succeed.
We therefore must adopt the right attitude
of combined self-assurance
and humble awareness of where we stand.

'Lord, you are our Goodness, through overflowing goodness and all in yourself. Whereas I am the Wretchedness, through overflowing wretchedness all in myself.' Blessed Marguerite Porete of the Beguines

Lord, remind us that a time comes
when the master of the house will get up and lock the door.
We will know then
that we will find ourselves knocking on the door
and realising that it has been locked by the Master.
We will then say in a loud voice, Lord, open to us.
Remind us that at this point,
you will find that you have to answer us,
I don't know where you come from.
Then we will find ourselves saying,
we once ate and drank in your company
and you once taught in our streets.
You will then reply, I don't know where you come from.
You will then tell us in the fateful words of the psalm,
Away from me, all you wicked men and women.

'The Word was made flesh in the incarnation, but ever since we have tried to make that flesh into word again.' Cardinal Martini
Lord, we look forward to days when we will know
that there will be weeping and grinding of teeth
as we see Abraham and Isaac and Jacob
and all the prophets in the kingdom of God,
whereas we ourselves are turned outside.
On the other hand,
we will see men and women from east and west
and from north to south, come to take their places
at the feast of the kingdom of God.
Meanwhile we will find that we are no longer there.
Lord, help us to live in that spirit of humble following of Jesus.

'The religious have the best of God's messages but they present them in a very boring way.' G. K. Chesterton
Lord, remind us always
that those who we consider now last
will soon be first in your kingdom
whereas those now first will soon be last.
Help us to remember this sad reality
as we go through our ordinary lives,
so that we can be both truthful and very humble.

Twenty-Second Sunday in Ordinary Time

Gospel reading: Luke 14:1; 7-11

1On a sabbath day, Jesus had gone for a meal to the house of one of the leading Pharisees; and they watched him closely.

7He then told the guests a parable, because he had noticed how they picked the places of honour. He said this, 8'When someone invites you to a wedding feast, do not take your seat in the place of honour. A more distinguished person than you may have been invited, 9and the person who invited you both may come and say, 'Give up your place to this man.' And then, to your embarrassment, you would have to go and take the lowest place. 10No; when you are a guest, make your way to the lowest place and sit there, so that, when your host comes, he may say, 'My friend, move up higher.' In that way, everyone with you at the table will see you honoured. 11For everyone who exalts himself will be humbled, and the man who humbles himself will be exalted.'

The passage for our meditation today is difficult. It would seem that Jesus is encouraging us to be sly and manipulative, to take the lowest place so that we might be invited to go higher; the strategy that we in Trinidad know as 'playing dead to catch corbeau alive.' This, of course, cannot be the way to read this parable, since we know from the rest of the gospels that Jesus condemned all forms of deviousness, and St Paul captured his spirit by telling us that our 'yes' should be 'yes' and our 'no', 'no'.

We must know how to read parables; our problem is that parables are a way of teaching we are not accustomed to in our cultures. We are much more used to edifying stories which tell us of good people whom we are invited to imitate. But a parable is different: its purpose is to capture one particular moment, a deep moment when we experience grace in some way. If – as often happens in the parables of Jesus – there are details in the story, they are there to stimulate our imagination and so to help us re-live that moment in our own experience. Jesus' parables evoke for us the exciting moment when, for example, we suddenly realise that the long time of waiting for the crops to grow is over, and it is time to reap; the moment of hurt and resentment when we see someone who has worked only one hour

getting the same reward as we who worked all day in the sun;
the moment when we see clearly how mean we have been in
harbouring resentment at some little wrong that a friend has
done to us, although we have been greatly blessed in many
other ways.

Today's parable invites us to enter into two precious moments. Don't hurry; take each one separately and stay some time
with it. The first is in verses 8 and 9: we suddenly discover that
we have claimed for ourselves a place that is too high for us; we
are not as selfless, generous or compassionate as we thought we
were, while we see before us people who really possess these
qualities. We had accepted the role in which the community had
placed us – as priest or religious or 'prominent Catholic' – but in
a crisis our frailty is revealed to ourselves alone or to the community; to our embarrassment, we go and take the lowest place.
The parable is telling us that when grace comes into our lives it
is like that, it is always an opportunity for spiritual growth,
painful though it may be.

On the other hand, there is the experience of verse 10, that
touching moment that happens every once in a way, when we
are made to feel good about ourselves. We were looking after a
sick relative, minding a neighbour's child, working hard at our
job, doing it all without fuss but taking for granted that it was
the right thing to do; then a person, a Bible passage, or a spiritual
book showed us that we were doing something wonderful and,
in fact, living the story of Jesus.

The parable conveys exactly the atmosphere of the last judgement in Chapter 25 of St Matthew's gospel, where the virtuous
are quite surprised that their little acts of kindness were really
done to Jesus, and the wicked suddenly realise that they had neglected to serve him. Today's passage shows us that it is not
merely a teaching about the last judgement, but about what always happens when God touches us.

Be careful about applying verses 8 and 9 to others, as you
could easily fall into a self-righteous or judgemental reading.
But feel very free in letting verse 10 remind you of people you
admire, the kind of people who, when you praise them are surprised or even embarrassed – 'I was only doing what anyone in
my position would do.' The parable is telling you to think of

someone like that, and you will have an idea of what it is to be a Christian. Enter into the concreteness of the parable, remembering people whom you don't have to worry about when you invite them to your home or to a function; you know that they will be happy with whatever they find. Enter into their spirituality, the deep attitude which makes them like that, and thank God for them.

You might like to identify with the host in the parable, the people in your life who have shown you your weaknesses and made you take the lowest place where you belonged. At the time, you were angry with them, but today, as you meditate on the passage, you thank God that he sent them to help you grow spiritually. Thank him too for the one who invited you to see your greatness and to experience yourself honoured by all those who sit at table with you, your family or church community. Admire the insightfulness of the host, and his courage; this will suggest to you the role of the Christian in a community, or that of the church in society – to expose all forms of phoniness on the one hand, and on the other to invite little people to take their rightful place of honour, even if it means that those in high places will be embarrassed.

The passage ends with verse 11, another of Jesus' great sayings; we know that the first Christians loved it very much because it is found several times in the gospels, and in different contexts. There is no need to join it to the parable (although you may find that it sums up its message for you); you can concentrate on entering into its truth in a new and deeper way than ever before, and this could be the special grace that God has in store for you this Sunday.

The saying is sometimes taken to mean that there is something wrong in holding high office, or even in wanting to, or that it is necessarily virtuous to chose a lowly position in a community. In fact, choosing a lowly position could be an evasion of a responsibility which God wants us to assume. There are many passages in the Bible which correct such false interpretations. In any case, the saying is not dealing with that question at all.

We can interpret those who humble themselves as the little people in a community, those who go about their business even though they are not given due recognition. Those who exalt themselves would be those who consider themselves superior to others, and oppress them with their superior attitudes. The saying then becomes a prayer of thanksgiving like the Magnificat, or a prayer of trust, leaving to God the work of establishing his kingdom of peace and justice. It also becomes a challenge to us to play our part in correcting the imbalances of society.

You can also read the saying as a paradoxical law of spiritual growth. There is a strong tendency in our culture to be self-centred in our desire to grow spiritually. Jesus is telling us that if we try too much to measure our spiritual growth, we end up regressing. If we leave ourselves in God's hands, letting him do the exalting, as it were, we give ourselves space to grow. St Francis expressed this attitude perfectly when he said: 'What I am before God is what I am, and nothing more.' Don't remain abstract at this point: remember the moment when you understood this law, and moved away from preoccupation with yourself, and thank God for sending you Jesus to teach you through a friend or a spiritual guide. Pray for someone who is making that same mistake, that they may experience the 'exaltation' that flows from total trust in God's love, which is what the saying means by humbling ourselves.

Look back, then, to verse 1 in the passage, and see Jesus in that hostile environment, perfectly free, not afraid to accept an invitation to have a meal with people who he knew did not share his values. The secret to his freedom is, of course, precisely the attitude he taught in this parable: he knew that he was in his Father's hands, and that was sufficient for him. Compare him with those others who were picking the places of honour, and recognise two attitudes which we have all adopted at times, and which we have seen in our communities.

* * *

Lord, when on a sabbath day,
we go for a meal to some of our leading Pharisees,
we know we will be watched very closely.
Remind us that at such times,
we must tell others how we must all be happy
to sit at a lowly place at any assembly.
Truly those who exalt themselves will be humbled,
whereas those who humble themselves will be truly exalted.

Twenty-Third Sunday in Ordinary time

Gospel reading: Luke 14:25-33

25*Great crowds accompanied him on his way and he turned and spoke to them.* 26*'If any man comes to me without hating his father, mother, wife, children, brothers, sisters, yes and his own life too, he cannot be my disciple.* 27*Anyone who does not carry his cross and come after me cannot be my disciple.* 28*And indeed, which of you here, intending to build a tower, would not first sit down and work out the cost to see if he had enough to complete it?* 29*Otherwise, if he laid down the foundation and then found himself unable to finish the work, the onlookers would all start making fun of him and saying,* 30*"Here is a man who started to build and was unable to finish."* 31*Or again, what king marching to war against another king would not first sit down and consider whether with ten thousand men he could stand up to the other who advanced against him with twenty thousand?* 32*If not, then while the other king was still a long way off, he would send envoys to sue for peace.* 33*So in the same way, none of you can be my disciple unless he gives up all his possessions.'*

The passage is in three movements:
- verse 25: the framework of the passage;
- verses 26, 27 and 33: the challenge to radical discipleship;
- verses 28 to 32: the practical approach to discipleship.

Discipleship of Jesus takes many forms and we interpret this passage in the light of the particular form of discipleship to which we have committed ourselves – marriage, parenting, friendship, career, religious life or priesthood. We think of other commitments we and others make: to social change for example – bringing about reconciliation between ethnic groups or religions, or reforming economic, educational or political systems, locally or internationally.

Jesus' language is startling at a first reading, harsh even, for example its stress on 'hating' and the need to give up 'all one's possessions'. Our meditation must feel the passion of Jesus as well as uplift us. The secret is to let the passage speak to our experiences of grace, of Jesus alive in the world today, and in each of us too, to the extent that we are his presence for others. It will also be a call to conversion of course, because we are often not like him.

For example, the passage invites us to celebrate those people who, when we were embarking on a career, joining a political movement, getting married, came straight with us. They told us: don't enter into it unless you feel willing and able for the sacrifices involved. Their words seemed harsh at the time and in any case we were so committed that we didn't pay them much heed. Now we are deeply grateful to them. They were Jesus at work in our lives.

Note that Jesus 'turned and spoke to them'. He speaks from personal experience. The choices he is asking from his followers he has made himself – and is glad he did.

Many leaders today (even in the church) are afraid of losing their followers, the 'great crowds who accompany them', so rather than challenge them, they feed them with empty slogans which pander to their worst instincts, for example their feelings of superiority to others. Or else they make demands on others that they do not live up to themselves. We celebrate leaders like Jesus.

We can shift the focus of our meditation from the person of Jesus to the process of decision making or coming to maturity which he calls us to. We all experience turning points in our lives, when in response to an inner call, we make choices which bring us to a new level of maturity. These moments of grace always involve finding our true identity by renouncing attachments – to people, projects, ideas, institutions. We decide to 'carry our own cross,' to discover our own destiny, the greatness to which we have been called.

So long as we derive our identity from others, even those closest to us, we remain immature.

Modern psychology has reinforced this teaching of Jesus:

'Before individuality can come there must be psychological differentiation. The unconscious identification with others must be broken, and each one must recognize his or her uniqueness.' *John A. Sanford, Jungian analyst and author*

The journey to maturity is on-going. As children, we find our points of reference in parents and possessions. As we get older we naturally transfer our dependence to other intimate relationships, from mother and father, brothers and sisters, to teachers, spouse, children, maybe work place, community, church, institution – a 'corporate self-image.' All the time we remain dependent on someone or something for our identity. The moment of maturity comes when we take the risk of stepping out into the unknown – we 'hate our own life too'. Up to then we are not mature, 'cannot be disciples'. Maturity brings freedom in our relationships, freedom from what others think of us, and freedom to let others discover who they are, apart from us.

Remaining faithful to our commitments requires many renunciations:
- familiar forms of prayer;
- childhood images of God;
- rules and regulations;
- identity that comes from belonging to a group, a movement, an institution, a political party;
- comforting passages in the scriptures;
- inward-looking cozy communities;

these can all be 'possessions' and eventually we realise that we must 'give them up'.

We celebrate heroes we have known who found the courage to 'give up' some deep-seated 'possessions,' taboos and silences they once clung to out of fear or a false sense of loyalty:
- battered women give up their sense of shame and share their stories with others;
- victims of rape, incest, or child abuse denounce their abusers;
- parents seek help for crippled, deformed or retarded children they had been hiding in their homes;
- citizens take the risk of going against their governments' oppressive policies;
- church members speak out against injustice in their communities;
- an Israeli speaks up for Palestinians, a Northern Ireland Catholic for Protestants, a Sicilian against the mafia.

The two parables in verses 28-30 and 31-32 are very touching, but we must interpret them according to the spirituality of Jesus. They must not make us afraid to take risks, for example, or weigh us down with guilt at our failures. Situate the parables in the context of Jesus 'turning around' and sharing his experience with compassion, remembering his temptations in the wilderness. We must feel the pathos of the 'onlookers all starting to make fun of the man'. It is not condemning but saying, 'I so want to spare you that'. But there is also the hint that we cannot escape such mocking. We remember the many references to 'those who scoff' in the psalms, and the chief priests mocking Jesus on Calvary because he 'started to build and was unable to finish'.

The parable of the king reminds us of moments when we feel discouraged and unable to continue in our commitments. The odds seem too great, we become aware that there are twenty thousand men against us whereas we only have ten thousand, and so we are tempted to 'send envoys to sue for peace' – like Jesus at Gethsemane. But God sends us some Jesus – or an angel – who reminds us that the commitment we made really requires that we 'give up all our possessions'.

The journey to discipleship is truly a wonderful adventure. We ask God to continue sending Jesus to lead us and all humanity along the way.

* * *

Lord, we remember with gratitude those people who,
as we were walking behind them,
turned and spoke words that seemed harsh at the time,
telling us
    - to break ties;
    - to step out in faith;
    - to harden our hearts;
    - not to be afraid to cause pain to the people we love.
By their words and example,
they gave us a new sense of freedom,
opened within us new sources of creativity,
helped us to be true to our deeper selves.

'We cannot discover new oceans unless we dare to lose sight of the shore.'
Lord, to discover new oceans, our young people must often
let go of father, mother, brothers and sisters,
yes and their own image of themselves too.

We thank you for great parents and teachers
who when their children want to continue accompanying them,
turn and speak to them as Jesus did,
telling them that they must not be afraid
to hurt those who are dear to them,
but must take up their own crosses
so that they can be truly his disciples.

Lord, we pray for young people.
So often those they accompany on their way
lead them in wrong directions;
they are subjected to pressure from peer groups, consumerism,
materialism, fads and fashions.
Send them leaders like Jesus who, as they walk ahead of them,
will turn and challenge them
  - to become the great people you want them to be,
  - to harden their hearts so that they can follow their own
  path,
  - not to be afraid to give up their feelings of security and assume their responsibilities.

Lord, as we look back on our lives
we see projects that we started,
for which we laid a foundation,
and which, later, we found ourselves unable to finish:
  - a marriage broke up;
  - we dropped out of school or college;
  - we left the religious life or the priesthood;
  - gave up a political commitment that was too demanding;
  - stopped meditating.
We hear voices, some of them within our own hearts,
making fun of us, saying, 'Here are people who started to build
and were unable to finish';
and indeed we had not sat down and worked out the cost
to see if we had the resources to complete what we had begun.
But we know that you are there with us,
and that the need to achieve is one
of the possessions you want us to give up.

Lord, we think today of those who are discouraged:
- parents bringing up their children;
- employers trying to work for good industrial relations;
- leaders challenging a church community to become involved in the secular world.
They feel like a king
who is marching out with ten thousand followers
and having to stand up to an opponent
who is advancing against him with twenty thousand;
they are inclined to sue for peace
even though their opponents are still a long way off.
Send them Jesus to remind them
that unless they are willing to give up
the desire for quick results,
and carry the cross of failure, they cannot be his disciples.

Twenty-Fourth Sunday in Ordinary Time

Gospel reading: Luke 15:1-10

¹*The tax collectors and the sinners, meanwhile, were all seeking the company of Jesus to hear what he had to say,* ²*and the Pharisees and the scribes complained, 'This man' they said 'welcomes sinners and eats with them.'* ³*So he spoke this parable to them:*

⁴*'What man among you with a hundred sheep, losing one, would not leave the ninety-nine in the wilderness and go after the missing one till he found it?* ⁵*And when he found it, would he not joyfully take it on his shoulders* ⁶*and then, when he got home, call together his friends and neighbours? "Rejoice with me," he would say "I have found my sheep that was lost."* ⁷*In the same way, I tell you, there will be more rejoicing in heaven over one repentant sinner than over ninety-nine virtuous men who have no need of repentance.* ⁸*Or again, what woman with ten drachmas would not, if she lost one, light a lamp and sweep out the house and search thoroughly till she found it?* ⁹*And then, when she had found it, call together her friends and neighbours? "Rejoice with me," she would say, "I have found the drachma I lost."* ¹⁰*In the same way, I tell you, there is rejoicing among the angels of God over one repentant sinner.'*

Verses 1 to 3 give us an overall picture of the kind of person Jesus was – and thus an image of God.

We follow that path in our meditation: we recognise and celebrate human beings who were images of Jesus for us, and allow them to reveal God to us.

In meditating on these verses, we are free to identify either

(a) with Jesus: who are the great people who draw the outcasts and are criticised for it? or

(b) with the 'tax collectors and sinners:' when were we deeply touched at being welcomed by someone we looked up to? or

(c) with 'the scribes and Pharisees': when did we criticise a member of our community for associating with people we considered 'tax collectors and sinners'?

We must enter into the literary form of the parables, experiencing them as dramatic, imaginative stories, so that we can identify with the characters at the feeling level.

The two parables are complementary in that the 'seeker' is male in the first parable and female in the second. Both are wonderfully portrayed as well-rounded persons, however – no stereotyping here. The shepherd is very tender, the woman efficient and business-like.

Though the 'seekers' are the main characters, we can be imaginative enough to identify with the lost sheep or the lost coin.

Don't hurry your meditation. Linger over the two movements. The search first, the feeling of being lost on the one hand, the frantic search on the other. Then there is the moment of finding, which can also be meditated on from the perspective of either the finder or the found. Both parables stress that the joy is not private but poured out and shared with the whole community.

In the well known poem 'Footprints', a man dreams that as he walks through life, there are two sets of footprints behind him – except at those times when he feels lost. He questions the Lord who replies: 'During your times of trial, there is only one set of footprints, because at those times I carried you.'

'There is greater rejoicing... ' In the gospels Jesus always seems to prefer sinners to the just. We must not try to understand this (or explain it) rationally. Jesus invites us to follow the parable way, remembering our experience as parents or teachers. Like every loving parent, God loves his children equally and always, but he knows that there are times when they feel 'lost', and are in greater need of care and reassurance than the others.

The sheep that was lost had broken away from the herd, symbolising those who take risks, dare to question, to seek new ways. The 'ninety-nine who have no need of repentance' are the complacent, they do not trust enough to take risks. They do not get lost but they achieve nothing either. No wonder there is 'greater rejoicing' over 'the lost'. Experience teaches us too that those who think they have it all do not learn. We know the paradox: we can only be found when we are lost.

* * *

Lord, we remember times when we found ourselves in company
where we felt out of place:
    - poor in a wealthy home,
    - young in the company of adults,
    - our first day at work and we were lonely and alienated,
    - something we had done came to light making us feel
    ashamed of ourselves,
    - a conversation was way above our heads.
You sent someone like Jesus who gave us a warm welcome
and made us feel at home, ate with us,
conversed with us as equals,
just as important as the scribes and Pharisees who were around.

Lord, forgive us for the times when we are content
to remain with those of our social class,
race, religion, academic world.
We thank you for people
who break out of these narrow confines
and mix freely with those whom we tend to ignore.
Our first response is to be surprised even angry, to complain.
We recognise now that it is Jesus among us.

*'The sheep may be lost in fog or wandering aimlessly but the shepherd
is always in search of it. No matter how desperate our plight, we may
always rely on the love which will never tire of seeking us out, whatever may be the burden of sin or guilt we carry.'* Cardinal Basil Hume
Lord, we thank you for the times when we feel we are failures,
not worthy of being loved,
we withdraw from those closest to us, lost in self-pity,
like a sheep wandering around the hills,
or a coin on the floor hidden in the dust,
and you send us people who seek us out
– spiritual directors, parents, teachers, friends.
They leave their ninety-nine other preoccupations
and give us their undivided attention,
take our burdens on themselves,
like a shepherd taking a lost sheep on his shoulders.
They seem so happy to be with us
that we feel we are more important to them

than all those who never gave them any trouble.
Lord, these people reveal to us how you love us.

Lord, we are so afraid of taking risks,
of being separated from the rest of the flock, of getting lost.
Fear is the reason why we find it difficult
   - to forgive those who have hurt us;
   - to reach out to those of a different race or ethnic group;
   - to explore new ways of prayer;
   - to commit ourselves to a new relationship.
Remind us that we can trust life, people, you in the last resort.
Even if we get lost, you always send someone,
a word, to come after us,
even if this means leaving the ninety-nine in the wilderness.

Lord, we thank you that you understand us parents.
You know how we fuss over the one child
who is always in trouble
like a woman who has lost her money and lights a lamp
and sweeps out her house,
searching thoroughly until she finds it.
Our other children complain
that we are always leaving them in the lurch
and going after the one who is missing.
But it is not that we don't love them equally;
we would do the same for every one of them.
It is just that, here and now,
we feel more joy over the one child we can bring back
than over the others who are safe.
People who are ruled by logical argument,
like the Pharisees and the scribes,
cannot understand – but you do,
and all of us who have experienced love.

Lord, our world is run by cold, calculating logic,
so that losing one sheep is of little importance
if we have ninety-nine others in the wilderness;
and it is not worth lighting a lamp, sweeping out the house
and searching thoroughly for one drachma out of ten.

You want us build a different world,
founded on love,
where there is more rejoicing over one repentant person
than over ninety-nine virtuous ones
who have no need of repentance,
and great rejoicing among your angels
over one person who was lost and is now found.

Twenty-Fifth Sunday in Ordinary time

Gospel reading: Luke 16:1-13

[1]Jesus said to his disciples: 'There was a rich man and he had a steward who was denounced to him for being wasteful with his property. [2]He called for the man and said, 'What is this I hear about you? Draw me up an account of your stewardship because you are not to be my steward any longer.' [3]Then the steward said to himself, 'Now that my master is taking the stewardship from me, what am I to do? Dig? I am not strong enough. Go begging? I should be too ashamed. [4]Ah, I know what I will do to make sure that when I am dismissed from office there will be some to welcome me into their homes.' [5]Then he called his master's debtors one by one. To the first he said, 'How much do you owe my master?' [6]'One hundred measures of oil' was the reply. The steward said, 'Here, take your bond; sit down straight away and write fifty.' [7]To another he said, 'And you, sir, how much do you owe?' 'One hundred measures of wheat' was the reply. The steward said, 'Here, take your bond and write eighty.' [8]The master praised the dishonest steward for his astuteness. For the children of this world are more astute in dealing with their own kind than are the children of light. [9]And so I tell you this: use money, tainted as it is, to win you friends, and thus make sure that when it fails you, they will welcome you into the tents of eternity. [10]The man who can be trusted in little things can be trusted in great; the man who is dishonest in little things will be dishonest in great. [11]If then you cannot be trusted with money, that tainted thing, who will trust you with genuine riches? [12]And if you cannot be trusted with what is not yours, who will give you what is your very own? [13]No servant can be the slave of two masters: he will either hate the first and love the second, or treat the first with respect and the second with scorn. You cannot be the slave both of God and of money.'

The passage is in two movements:
- verses 1 to 7, the parable;
- verses 8 to 13, a collection of six sayings of Jesus, all connected with the parable.

Most people find this parable one of the most difficult to interpret, seeming to condone the dishonesty of the steward. The main problem here is our tendency to read the gospels and the parables particularly, in a rational, moralising way. We then find ourselves passing judgement on the parables: 'a touching story but ...' With this approach to our parable we have to do mental gymnastics to explain how the master could 'praise the dishonest steward'.

We are not meant to read parables in such a heady, moralising (basically self-righteous) way. We must enter freely into them ('with a willing suspension of disbelief'), get a feel for the characters, and gradually let them reveal some deep lesson about human living.

With this parable, for example, we must identify with the steward, allow him to become a person whom we feel we would like to praise, just like the master in the parable did.

If we look at him in that perspective, we find that he is very likeable, not efficient – 'wasteful' as the parable says – but very likeable. We imagine a person who knows how to enjoy life. He doesn't like hard work – 'Dig? I am not strong enough' – but he likes people and enjoys the company of his friends.

Note that he didn't take the master's money for himself, he was 'wasteful' in that he did not force his master's debtors to pay. Even his dishonesty was not for himself but for the debtors.

The steward in other words is exactly the kind of free person that Jesus liked, the tax collectors and sinners he kept company with. He much preferred them to the upright but very boring and self-righteous Pharisees.

Once we have identified the steward we interpret the seven sayings in the light of his character.

In verse 8, it is said that he is 'astute' meaning that he has his values right. In terms of the parable, the false value is 'property,' the true value is making friends.

Verse 9 says that money has its value but then explains that its value emerges only when we put it at the disposal of our friends. The 'tents of eternity' means friendship which lasts.

Verses 9 to 12 then tease out the difference between false and true values, 'little things' and 'great things' (verse 10), tainted and genuine riches (verse 11), what is 'not yours' and what is 'your very own' (verse 12).

In verse 13 the terms 'mammon', or 'money', stand for material things, 'God' is the truth.

Lord, we thank you for free-spirited people you send us
in our families, workplaces,
parish communities, neighbourhoods.
Like the steward in Jesus' parable,
they are often labeled wasteful or dishonest but, like the master,
we feel admiration for them,
recognising that they know how to deal with people
better than we church people
who are supposed to be children of the light.
So often we make a fuss about having accounts right,
and everything in our house in the right place,
whereas for them it is people who count.
We end up respected but lonely;
they however, even though earthly success fails them,
win themselves many friends
who welcome them into their hearts
and are forever faithful to them.
They value secondary virtues as secondary not primary,
– punctuality, good order, neatness, obedience to authorities –
but they can be trusted to value what is truly important
– courtesy to the poor, trust, the willingness to admit mistakes.
They know that power, popularity and influence
are always tainted, and not to be made much of
– just like money;
they can be trusted with genuine riches
like good friends, children, health, nature.
They set no great store by things
like clothes, fancy houses and cars
which are not part of the people who own them;
they have a good share of what is their very own
– honesty, sincerity, integrity, openness.
They know that in life we have to choose our values.
We cannot have two sets of priorities;
if we try, we end up not making one of them a priority.
They are not subject to any material thing,
truth is their only master
and they find freedom in being its servants.

Twenty-Sixth Sunday in Ordinary Time

Gospel reading: Luke 16:19-31

19Jesus said to the Pharisees: 'There was a rich man who used to dress in purple and fine linen and feast magnificently every day. 20And at his gate there lay a poor man called Lazarus, covered with sores, 21who longed to fill himself with the scraps that fell from the rich man's table. Dogs even came and licked his sores. 22Now the poor man died and was carried away by the angels to the bosom of Abraham. The rich man also died and was buried. 23In his torment in Hades he looked up and saw Abraham a long way off with Lazarus in his bosom. 24So he cried out, "Father Abraham, pity me and send Lazarus to dip the tip of his finger in water and cool my tongue, for I am in agony in these flames." 25"My son," Abraham replied, "remember that during your life good things came your way, just as bad things came the way of Lazarus. Now he is being comforted here while you are in agony. 26But that is not all: between us and you a great gulf has been fixed, to stop anyone if he wanted to, crossing from our side to yours, and to stop any crossing from your side to ours." 27The rich man replied, "Father, I beg you then to send Lazarus to my father's house, 28since I have five brothers, to give them warning so that they do not come to this place of torment too." 29"They have Moses and the prophets," said Abraham, "let them listen to them." 30"Ah no, father Abraham," said the rich man, "but if someone comes to them from the dead, they will repent." 31Then Abraham said to him, "If they will not listen either to Moses or to the prophets, they will not be convinced even if someone should rise from the dead".'

This Sunday's passage is entirely taken up with one parable. It is in three sections – each one is a story in itself, so you can remain with any one of them:
- verses 19 to 22: an introductory scene ending with the death of both Lazarus and the rich man;
- verses 23 to 26: a first dialogue between the rich man and Abraham;
- verses 27 to 31: a second dialogue between them.

All but one of the Sunday gospel passages for the next few weeks include a parable. It is therefore good to remember the special kind of teaching that a parable is, a kind of teaching that is not common in our culture.

We are accustomed to moralising stories, in which the point of the story is to exhort us to imitate the hero or heroine. A parable is not meant to work like that. Its method is to evoke a personal response to the story: what a surprise that was! or, what an unexpected ending! Then it says to us: remember an experience like that and you will know what happens when God comes into people's lives.

As in every story, you must find yourself identifying with one of the characters; for example, in this parable there are three characters – the rich man, Lazarus, and Abraham.

A reminder for this parable: all Bible meditation must start from experience. Therefore do not read this parable first of all as something that happened in the next life, because you have no experience of that. The parable may well lead you to conclude something about the next life, but you mustn't start there.

* * *

Lord, there are times when we feel very lonely,
ignored by everyone,
as if we were at the gate of a very wealthy man,
longing to fill ourselves with scraps from his table.
But you lead us from there to an experience of security:
    - a moment of deep prayer;
    - we feel loved by our family;
    - we find ourselves in a group which shares our values.
We feel as if we had been gathered
into the bosom of our ancestors,
safe from all those who would send us here and there
for their own purposes,
as safe as if a great gulf had been fixed between us
to stop anyone who wanted to
from crossing from our side to theirs,
and to stop anyone crossing from their side to ours.
Thank you, Lord.

Lord, remorse is a terrible thing.
It is being in agony in flames of fire,

seeing those we have wronged a long way off,
longing to have them dip their finger in water
and cool our tongue,
and finding that between us and them
a great gulf has been fixed
to stop any crossing from their side to ours.
Preserve us, Lord.

Lord, we pray for parents today,
that they may teach right values to their children,
teaching them not to set their hearts
on purple clothes and fine linen
nor on feasting magnificently every day,
because these things die and are buried,
but to reverence poor people
because one day they will be carried
away by angels to the bosom of Abraham.

*'We must build a world where freedom is not an empty word and where
the poor man Lazarus can sit down at the same table with the rich
man.'* Pope Paul VI
Lord, when we look around at the world today, what do we see?
Rich nations dressed in purple and fine linen,
feasting magnificently every day,
while at their very gates lie poor nations,
covered with sores and longing to fill themselves
with scraps from the tables of the rich,
dogs even come and lick their sores.
Lord, we pray that your church may continue to call the world
to repentance as Jesus did.

*'The moment we cease to hold each other,
the moment we break faith with one another,
the sea engulfs us and the light goes out.'* James Baldwin
Lord, whenever the time comes
that rich people dress in purple and fine linen
and feast magnificently every day,
while the poor lie at their gates unattended,
their only future is to die and be buried.

Twenty-Seventh Sunday in Ordinary Time

Gospel reading: Luke 17:5-10

5*The apostles said to the Lord. 'Increase our faith.' 6The Lord replied, 'Were your faith the size of a mustard seed you could say to this mulberry tree, "Be uprooted and planted in the sea," and it would obey you. 7Which of you, with a servant ploughing or minding sheep, would say to him when he returned from the fields, "Come and have your meal immediately"? 8Would he not be more likely to say, "Get my supper laid; make yourself tidy and wait on me while I eat and drink. You can eat and drink yourself afterwards"? 9Must he be grateful to the servant for doing what he was told? 10So with you: when you have done all you have been told to do, say, "We are merely servants; we have done no more than our duty".'*

This Sunday's passage is in two clearly distinct sections:
- verses 5 to 6 – a teaching on faith; and
- verses 7 to 10 – a parable on humble service.

If you decide to meditate on the first section, enter into the movement of the story, identifying with the request of the apostles as well as with Jesus' response. Be careful how you handle the obvious exaggeration in the saying: remain faithful to the dramatic promise, but at the same time let your meditation be rooted in actual experience.

If you are meditating on the parable, remember the kind of teaching a parable is. This warning is specially important here as we could draw wrong conclusions from this parable – that God is a harsh taskmaster, for example, or that employers should treat their employees as the parable suggests.

* * *

Lord, one of the marks of our modern culture
is that we are always looking for more things,
more knowledge, more money, and more energy,
so naturally we look for more faith as well.
But you teach us that true faith is based on reality
and this means accepting our lack of courage,
our regrets and our fears,

and that in fact our faith is as small as a mustard seed.
With this kind of honesty we can achieve great things,
even to say to a mulberry tree,
'Be uprooted and planted in the sea,'
and it will obey us.

*'One person who can express ahimsa in life exercises a force superior to
all the forces of brutality.'* Gandhi
Lord, nowadays when people want to move trees
they call in a bulldozer,
and when they want to influence people they call in armies;
so we end up thinking that all life's problems can be solved
once we have machines that are powerful enough.
We thank you for the great people of our time,
people like Gandhi, Mother Teresa,
Nelson Mandela, Danilo Dolci,
who remind us, as Jesus did,
that virtue has greater power than any machine,
and that if we have faith we can say to great trees,
'Be uprooted and planted in the sea,' and they will obey us.

Lord, we remember with gratitude people we have known
who have done good work without any fuss:
    - good neighbours,
    - those who care for the sick and the retarded,
    - parents,
the kind of people who when they had worked hard all day
and returned home,
took it for granted that they must get supper laid,
make themselves tidy and wait on others
while they ate and drank,
content that they themselves would eat and drink afterwards.

Lord, help those of us who are involved
in training young people not to pamper them,
giving them the illusion that in life
we get quick rewards for our efforts.
Help us rather to challenge them as Jesus has challenged us,
showing them that if we want to do anything worthwhile in life

– and that includes being good fathers and mothers –
we must be ready to work hard, and at the end of the day
not expect to have anyone say to us
'Come and have your meal immediately.'
We are more likely to hear that we must get supper laid,
make ourselves tidy, and wait on others
while they eat and drink
and only afterwards we will be able to drink and eat ourselves.

'There is another manner of loving which is when the soul seeks to
serve our Lord for nothing in return, for love alone, without demand-
ing to know the reason why, and without any reward of grace or glory.'
Beatrice of Nazareth
Lord, forgive us
that we turn our prayer life into bargaining with you,
expecting that because we have done your will, you will tell us,
'Come and have your meal immediately'.
Lead us to that prayer where we leave ourselves
totally in your hands,
and when we have done all we have been told to do,
we say, 'We are merely servants
who have done no more than our duty.'

Twenty-Eighth Sunday in Ordinary Time

Gospel reading: Luke 17:11-19

11On the way to Jerusalem, Jesus travelled along the border between Samaria and Galilee. 12As he entered one of the villages, ten lepers came to meet him. They stood some way off 13and called to him, 'Jesus! Master! Take pity on us.' 14When he saw them he said, 'Go and show yourselves to the priests.' Now as they were going away they were cleansed. 15Finding himself cured, one of them turned back praising God at the top of his voice 16and threw himself at the feet of Jesus and thanked him. The man was a Samaritan. 17This made Jesus say, 'Were not all ten made clean? The other nine, where are they? 18It seems that no one has come back to give praise to God, except this foreigner.' 19And he said to the man, 'Stand up and go your way. Your faith has saved you.'

This Sunday's reading, though seemingly straightforward, is in fact a combination of two separate stories:

- Jesus heals ten lepers (verses 11 to 14);
- the grateful Samaritan earns Jesus' praise and an additional healing (verses 15 to 19).

Modern scholarship has shown that the two stories were originally separate and were combined in one text only gradually and after some time. You are in line with the truth of the text therefore if you choose to focus on one story alone, the one which happens to touch you here and now.

A caution, however. Most people coming to church on this Sunday are looking for a comment on the story of the Samaritan, and those who give homilies must take this into consideration when choosing what topic they will share on. Those who are reading the passage for personal meditation do not have that kind of responsibility to the community and are free to focus on the other story – the healing of the lepers.

The lepers: verses 11-14

Leprosy in the gospels is symbolic of the situation from which God willed to rescue his people. It is so in two ways:

- it disfigured people;
- those suffering from it were considered unclean and kept away from the community.

Jesus' response to lepers invites us to celebrate those who act like him, towards us or others. It also calls us to repentance as individuals and as church communities – this is the role we should be playing in our communities and in society.

In your meditation remember 'lepers' in your family, neighbourhood, classroom, workplace, society – people who are looked down on because they are disfigured in some way, and also those who may not be physically disfigured but are considered 'unclean' for some other reason: the mentally ill; those suffering from AIDS; ex-prisoners; gays and lesbians in certain communities; Asians in many countries of the world since the September 11 attacks; immigrants and asylum seekers; people who belong to minority ethnic or racial groups.

The lepers in the gospel story cry out, 'Jesus! Master! Take pity on us.' The lepers of our experience also cry out, but they often do so in different ways:

a) they behave badly – children are rebellious; students are unruly in the classroom; gangs of youths engage in destructive behaviour; adults argue their point of view aggressively and even violently; they become alcoholics or give in to some form of addiction. The root cause in many cases is an inferiority complex; they feel that others look down on them, that they are 'lepers' in their families or neighbourhoods.

b) Often they are silently uncooperative and surly, engaging in what psychologists call 'passive aggression'. They refuse to come to church, to attend community meetings or to participate in family discussions.

The text says that Jesus 'saw' the lepers. The expression is significant; it says that whereas others simply passed by, he took note of their condition. Nowadays this would include interpreting the behaviour patterns mentioned above.

It is significant too that Jesus met the lepers 'as he travelled along the border between Samaria and Galilee'. It is only if we take the risk of 'travelling along the borders' of our communities that we will meet the lepers of our time.

The expression 'go and show yourselves to the priests' is also significant, especially today. In the time of Jesus, the priests were civil authorities so that the text simply meant 'go with confidence to the leaders of the community.' Today many 'lepers' are rejected by their church communities or religious groups; they internalise this rejection and end up having guilt feelings about themselves. Jesus people give them the assurance that they have the right to 'show themselves' to the 'priests' of their culture; these include all those who dictate religious attitudes – parents, teachers, parish lay leaders, the 'holy people' of the community.

'As they were going their way they were cleansed.' Jesus had worked a miraculous cure but the text hints that their setting out with confidence to 'show themselves to the priests' had a healing effect – which corresponds to our experience.

The grateful Samaritan

Homilists often lay stress on Jesus being 'hurt' by the nine who did not return to thank him. This is undoubtedly an aspect of the story and as such is a reminder of the humanity of Jesus – like us, he was hurt by ingratitude. But we should not make too much of it; that would be to go against Jesus' character. He was not the kind of person who would make a fuss about being thanked. We know people like that and we don't admire them. The point is not stressed in the text either – Jesus praised the Samaritan for coming back 'to praise God', not himself. Besides, last Sunday's gospel taught us not to look for thanks when we do good, since we are 'doing no more than our duty'. Jesus could not go against his own teaching.

We are more in line with the movement of the passage, then, to interpret the story as a meditation (starting with our own experience as always) on gratitude as a wonderful gift. The focus is not on Jesus but on the Samaritan. What a wonderful person! He reminds us of people who, having gone abroad or to university and become successful, go back to their home town and 'throw themselves at the feet' of their teachers and their community leaders. The passage invites us to celebrate such people, they are a real blessing!

'Finding themselves cleansed' is significant – humble people know that though they have worked hard for their success, luck has played a large part too. Jesus said to the Samaritan, 'Your faith has saved you,' which means something like 'your humble spirit has made you a secure person.' This also is the meaning of 'stand up and go your way.' People who know how to give thanks are well equipped to face the disappointments of life, they can 'stand up and go their way' with enthusiasm and energy. On the contrary, those who do not give thanks – 'complainers' – are forever disappointed by life and lack the energy to move forward. Jesus' words 'Where are the nine?' express his regret that they were losing out on something very precious. The fact that only one out of ten 'came back to give praise to God' reminds us that gratitude is a rare gift. This is particularly true of our modern Western culture; we are so surrounded by creature comforts that we take God's blessings for granted and do not 'come back to give praise to him'.

This holds for natural things like water, sunlight, clouds, mountains and rivers; for family, friends, neighbours and fellow workers; for good health, and for healthcare.

Samaritans in the gospel symbolise those who have experienced rejection in any form. The story tells us then that such people are naturally more inclined to be grateful. We can conclude that the most effective way to come to gratitude is to remember 'where we came from'. Moses made this point when he commanded the people to be compassionate to the stranger, reminding them, 'You too were strangers in Egypt.'

This approach is of course radically opposed to the condescension of 'aid to the poor countries of the world' that is so common today. We as a church are often guilty of a similar condescension in our relations with other religions.

* * *

'The important events in history are the thousands of humble actions that heal and reconcile.' Cardinal Arns

Lord, we think today
of the many lepers in our society who stand some way off
and call to those passing by, 'Master, take pity on us.'
We thank you for the Jesus people who notice them
as they travel along the borders of their societies
and tell them to go and show themselves
to the leaders of their communities.

Lord, our church has made many people feel unclean
- because of their sexual orientation;
- because their marriages broke up;
- because they became pregnant out of wedlock;
- because they gave up the priesthood or religious life;
- because members of their families are in prison or on drugs.
Send them spiritual guides like Jesus
who will see deeply into their condition
and tell them that they are not unclean,
and can go with confidence
and show themselves to the priests.
Once they know this, they will be cleansed as they go their way.

'Man is straighter when he bends and taller when he bows.'
G. K. Chesterton
Lord, one of the great sicknesses of our time
Is to have lost the art of giving thanks.
What a pity that so few people come back and give praise to you;
Like Jesus we wonder where are the others.
When we take your blessings for granted
we lose energy and enthusiasm.
It is only when we know
how to throw ourselves at the feet of those who help us
and give thanks
that we can really stand up with confidence and go our way.

*'You must not infringe on the rights of the foreigner or the orphan.
Remember that you were once a slave in Egypt and that the Lord your
God redeemed you from that.'* Deuteronomy 24:17-18
Lord, help us to come to those in need
without the slightest trace of condescension,
not as chosen people but as Samaritans
who know what it is to be in need ourselves
and have had to throw ourselves
at the feet of those who made us clean.

'There are things that can only be seen by eyes that have cried.'
Archbishop Christopher Munzihirwa, Jesuit Rwandan bishop killed in civil war
Lord, when we remember the pains we have suffered
we can stand up, like the Samaritan leper,
and follow the way of peace and reconciliation.

'We should look at green again and be startled anew, but not blinded,
by blue and yellow and red. Fairy tales help us to make this rediscov-
ery.' J. R. Tolkien
Lord, give us the heart of a child,
so that we may know how to come back and give thanks to you
for the simple things in life.

Twenty-Ninth Sunday in Ordinary time

Gospel reading: Luke 18:1-8

¹*Jesus told his disciples a parable about the need to pray continually and never lose heart.* ²*'There was a judge in a certain town,' he said 'who had neither fear of God nor respect for man.* ³*In the same town there was a widow who kept on coming to him and saying, "I want justice from you against my enemy!"* ⁴*For a long time he refused, but at last he said to himself, "Maybe I have neither fear of God nor respect for man,* ⁵*but since she keeps pestering me I must give this widow her just rights, or she will persist in coming and worry me to death".'* ⁶*And the Lord said, 'You notice what the unjust judge has to say?* ⁷*Now will not God see justice done to his chosen who cry to him day and night even when he delays to help them?* ⁸*I promise you, he will see justice done to them, and done speedily. But when the Son of Man comes, will he find any faith on earth?'*

Today's passage is in four movements:
- verse 1: introduction to the parable
- verses 2 to 5: the parable
- verses 6 to 8a: Jesus draws a conclusion from the parable
- verse 8b: a saying of Jesus, flowing from the parable.

At a first reading it is a teaching on prayer, 'the need to pray continually and never lose heart'. In the Bible, however, 'prayer' is always used in a wide sense to refer to our entire relationship with God, and indeed our spiritual life in general.

After last week's story of the grateful Samaritan, we return to the parable form of the previous weeks. We must once more remember the 'laws' for interpreting a parable, in particular that we must choose which character in the story we want to focus on. In this parable it is clearly the widow. The 'unjust judge' is the foil who makes her greatness stand out; he is not important in himself. We must certainly not identify him with God, as some do. He ends up – like God – giving justice to the widow, but that is the only resemblance.

The widow is in fact a wonderful person, one of the great characters of the gospels, indeed of the whole Bible. Like last week's grateful Samaritan, and like the humble servant of the week before, she will become real for us if we allow her to remind us of people we have known. We can then celebrate her and let her speak a message of repentance to us, both as individuals and as a church at every level: the universal church; our particular church, our diocese or the church of our nation; our local church, parish or small basic community within the parish.

The widow is poor. She cannot back her claims with money or influential people; her power lies entirely in her moral qualities, her passion and her perseverance. We remember people from poor communities (nations, or groups within a nation) who are extraordinarily courageous in 'seeking justice against their enemies.' For them justice takes many forms:
- getting their children into a good school;
- finding jobs for them after they have left school;
- finding money for their children's food or education;
- completing their homes;
- maintaining their health so that they continue to serve their families.

They 'persist in coming to'
- government offices;
- principals of schools;
- hospitals and doctors' offices.

They have little concern for
- what people think about them;
- how they appear to the general public;
- whether they are being a nuisance.

They show the same qualities in their relationship with God, storming heaven with their prayers, caring little if these are theologically correct.

The 'widows' of our experience are often communities:
- poor nations standing up for their rights before the world community;
- peace movements in Ireland, the Basque country, within the Israeli-Palestine conflict;
- movements representing the oppressed like the landless in Brazil.

Like the widow in the parable, they have no financial or military resources, but they persevere in 'seeking justice against their enemies,' confident that their cause will eventually triumph.

Jesus is not condescending to the poor. He draws his followers' attention to their plight, not to feel sorry for them, not even to help them, but to learn from (be converted, evangelised, by) them. We who reflect on these gospels today are often not in the situation of the widow. The gospel invites us to capture her spirit, making the journey from Luke's 'blessed are the poor' to Matthew's 'blessed are the poor in spirit'. We do this most effectively by entering into solidarity with the 'widows' of our society, joining one of their organisations or taking up their cause publicly.

The widow has two important lessons to teach us. First, she had no recourse to force because as a poor person force was not available to her. We must choose to be like her by renouncing violence in any form in our 'seeking for justice'. So too we are often lacking in passion in our search for justice. This is because injustice does not crowd us as it does poor people. We can survive without any dramatic change in our circumstances so we can afford to say, 'This is how life is,' and leave things like that. The poor are like the widow, they do not have that luxury; they seek justice with passion because for them it is a matter of life or death. By entering into solidarity with them we too learn to seek justice with passion.

We think of NGOs demonstrating against the world's economic system, against wrong development projects, as they have done in recent years in Seattle, in Quebec, in Genoa, in Cancun. Most of the demonstrators are not poor themselves, but they have identified with the poor and in the process taken on the qualities of the widow in the parable:
- seeking justice with passion;
- refusing to be put off by lack of success;
- renouncing violence.

There are times when destiny arranges for us to share the experience of the poor:
- we lose our wealth;
- we become ill and must fall back on the facilities (or lack of them) of the poor;
- we are victims of violent crime – a common occurrence for poor people. The attacks of September 11 are an example.

We turn these situations into moments of grace when we imitate the widow in the parable (and those we meet in real life).

Verses 6 to 8a: If we are starting from experience – as we must – we will have to interpret Jesus' promise that 'he will see justice done to them and speedily'. It certainly does not happen literally. I suggest two possible interpretations (you will probably find others):

a) We take 'justice' as the objective righting of wrongs. This is often a long time coming, but when it does come, we are so relieved (and surprised) that we forget the long wait; it appears to come 'speedily'.

b) We can apply the saying to spiritual growth. Once we develop the right attitude then we 'speedily' know that our prayers are answered, according to Jesus' teaching that once we knock the door is already opened. We celebrate the times when we (or others) have experienced this.

Verse 8b: We are invited to identify with Jesus as he utters the anguished cry, 'When the Son of Man comes, will he find any faith on earth?' It is a 'feeling' statement, and we must read it as such, not rationalise it.

We can interpret it in two ways:

a) How few people have faith like that widow! Since we have total confidence that the Son of Man will in fact come, it is an expression of regret. What a pity that so few people are willing to wait!

b) How long it takes before the Son of Man comes! I wonder if anyone will wait that long. When we feel those reactions within ourselves, it means that Jesus is at work in us.

* * *

'Blessed are those who hunger and thirst for justice, they shall have their fill.' Matthew 5:6

Lord, we thank you for the widows of the modern world
who persist in looking for justice:
- ethnic minorities throughout the world;
- women looking for equal opportunities in society;
- those who work for land reform in Brazil;
- Caribbean parents giving up everything to secure a good education for their children.

We thank you that they continue to cry out night and day,
even when you delay to help them,
trusting in your promise to see justice done to them,
and done speedily.
They assure us that when the Son of Man comes
he will find faith on earth.

'No one possesses the truth, everyone seeks it.' Bishop Pierre Claverie of
Algeria, martyred in 1996
Lord, help us to seek the truth humbly and perseveringly,
like the widow in the gospel, crying out day and night
even when it delays in revealing itself to us.

'In this Holy City of three mighty religions, no one seems to have the
faith to make the peaceful decision.' David Rudder, calypsonian in Trinidad,
commenting on the situation in Jerusalem
Lord, we thank you for those who are working for peace
    - between Israelis and Palestinians;
    - in the Basque country, in the Congo;
    - between Muslims and Christians worldwide;
    - in the campaign against terrorism.
We thank you that they keep on coming and saying
 'We do not want war,'
continue crying to you day and night
even when you delay to help them.

Lord, we have created a civilisation
in which self-interest is the highest value,
and competition the main incentive to progress.
The ideal is to have neither fear of you nor respect for man.
Forgive us that as a church we have given up hope
that things could be different,
and even say that you want them to be as they are.
We pray that your church may be like the widow,
always coming back in search of new solutions,
with the confidence that if we do not meet with success,
it is merely that you are delaying to help us,
for the poor are your chosen ones
and your will is to see justice done to them and done speedily.

'All holy desires grow by delays.' St Gregory
Lord, many religion teachers offer people
a naïve teaching on prayer, making it seem easy,
as if we merely have to ask for things and we get them.
Help us to share with others the teaching of Jesus
on the need to pray continually and never lose heart.
Remind us that when you delay to help us
you ensure that there will always be faith on earth.

'God said, "If it is I who allow you to be wounded so badly, do you not believe that I will heal you most lovingly in the very same hour?"'
Mechtild of Magdeburg
Lord, there are times when we experience you as a hard judge
and we are poor widows who must keep coming to you,
demanding justice against those who oppress us.
Lead us deeper into ourselves
where we can experience that we are your chosen ones
and you will see justice done to us and done speedily.

Lord, at this time in human history
many are seeking vengeance for terrorist attacks.
We pray that your church may be in word and in deed
the prophetic voice of Jesus
telling his disciples the parable of the widow
seeking justice against her enemies.

Thirtieth Sunday in Ordinary Time

Gospel text: Luke 18:9-14

9Jesus spoke the following parable to some people who prided them-selves on being virtuous and despised everyone else. 10'Two men went up to the Temple to pray, one a Pharisee, the other a tax collector. 11The Pharisee stood there and said this prayer to himself, "I thank you, God, that I am not grasping, unjust, adulterous like the rest of mankind, and particularly that I am not like this tax collector here. 12I fast twice a week; I pay tithes on all I get." 13The tax collector stood some distance away, not daring even to raise his eyes to heaven; but he beat his breast and said, "God, be merciful to me, a sinner." 14This man, I tell you, went home again at rights with God; the other did not. For everyone who exalts himself will be humbled, but the man who humbles himself will be exalted.'

This Sunday's gospel reading is in three sections
  - verse 9, introduction to the parable;
  - verses 10-14a, the parable;
  - verse 14b, general saying of Jesus.
As always with gospel passages we are free either to focus on the sections independently or to see the connection between them so that each one serves as a guide for interpreting the others.

This is particularly true for verse 14b. It occurs twice in St Luke's gospel which indicates that it was a favourite saying of Jesus, or of the early church. We are in line with the movement of the passage then if we choose to meditate on it separately but it is also essential for a correct interpretation of the parable.

The parable of the Pharisee and the Publican is one of the great parables of Jesus, one that has affected the consciousness of people in every age. It is also one of the best known of the parables, and this can be a disadvantage for meditation: we are so accustomed to the story that our imaginations are dulled, and we read it superficially and abstractly. We must watch every word, therefore, and enter into the concreteness of the story, so that it can touch us as if we were reading it for the first time.

Unlike last week's parable which focused on the widow alone, this week's presents us with two characters, the Pharisee (story of sin) and the publican (story of grace) and they are of

228

equal importance. We (or others we have known) have lived both stories as individuals, but we have also lived them as communities – church, ethnic groups, nations and cultures. The human family as a whole has been both Pharisee and publican.

Our meditation then will lead to two responses:
- ask God's mercy for the sin;
- celebrate the grace.

We are also free to see a link between the two stories, and interpret the parable as tracing the journey from sin to grace. Consciousness of this journey will lead us to humble thanksgiving and also to petition that we (and others) will continue to make the journey.

At first glance the passage is a teaching about prayer but, as we saw with last week's passage, 'prayer' in the Bible includes all our deep attitudes – toward God, life, ourselves, one another, nature – and we must not restrict the scope of the passage. Like all gospel passages it is 'catholic' teaching, applicable to life at every level – spiritual growth, personal relationships, the workplace, politics, international trade, etc.

Verse 9: 'Jesus spoke this parable' must be read creatively. Jesus has many ways of 'speaking parables':
- a teacher (friend, neighbour, fellow worker, member of our family) teaches us a lesson;
- we meet an actual Pharisee or publican at home, in church, or at work;
- some humiliation reveals to us how much we have the spirit of the Pharisee.

The parable. As I explained above, both characters are of equal importance in this parable. You are free then to choose which of the two you want to focus on at this particular moment. Focusing on both at the same time is impossible if you are working through your imagination. You can combine the two in your meditation but must still take one at a time.

The Pharisee. Ironically, it is easy to fall into the trap of reading the parable self-righteously. You will avoid this in two ways:
- by recognising yourself in the Pharisee;
- by finding him a person you can sympathise with; if you see him only negatively, you are reading the parable self-righteously.

In fact the Pharisee of the parable is generally the kind of person we would consider 'good'. The text gives no indication that he was a hypocrite, as many Pharisees were. According to the text, he was upright and faithful to his religious duties. His two sins (they are always linked, both in the Bible and in real life) were that

- he did not humble himself (omission);
- he looked down on others (commission).

Remember a time when Jesus made you aware that (perhaps subtly) you, your community, or your family were taking pride in your high moral standards. He may have done this in different ways, some of them unexpected:

- one of your children or some member of the church community criticised you;
- you found yourself committing a sin you never thought you would;
- a failure showed you that you were not as efficient as you thought you were.

However it happened, you celebrate the moment of grace.

The Publican. He too must be correctly interpreted. In Christian spirituality, he is often represented as someone without self-esteem. Jesus could not have presented us with such a role model; this would go against his entire teaching. We avoid this false interpretation by reading this section in the light of verse 14b. We identify the publican with people we admire deeply, whom we have 'exalted' – parents, community leaders, entrepreneurs whose greatness is grounded in humility. They are self-confident but have no illusions about themselves and therefore do not despise others; they 'dare not raise their eyes to heaven', but do not grovel.

Verse 14b. Beware of reading this verse in the abstract. Enter into its movement, so that you feel

- the sadness of the first part: how sad that this person (or movement) had so much potential and then fell so low!
- the triumph of the second part: how wonderful that this person who had fallen so low rose so high!

Feel, too, the contrast between the two outcomes (taking one at a time as I explained for the Pharisee and the publican) each one highlighting the other. We should not rejoice that the proud are humbled, only feel sadness at what might have been if the Pharisee had been true to his best self.

The saying is expressed in the passive voice – 'will be humbled', 'will be exalted'. In the Bible these passives are often an act of respect for the transcendence of God but in fact refer to God's actions – 'God will humble', 'God will exalt'. We see the same thing in the petitions of the Our Father: 'hallowed be thy name, thy kingdom come, thy will be done' are calls on God to intervene in the world. Our meditation here can be a celebration of God (and godly people) seeking out the lowly and 'exalting' them. The expressions 'exalt himself' and 'humble himself' will then be interpreted in the light of the Father exalting Jesus as explained in Philippians 2:6-11. It is important to give a correct interpretation to the future tenses 'will be humbled' and 'will be exalted'. They can refer to the next life, but on condition that they are based on present experience. Our experience of the lowly being exalted points to (and promises) their final exaltation at the end of time.

* * *

'The line dividing good and evil cuts through the heart of every human being.' Solzhenitsyn
Lord, we thank you for those who like Jesus
remind us that we can never pride ourselves on being virtuous,
and that we cannot afford to despise anyone.

'Faith is to accept the fact that I am accepted in my total unacceptability.'
Paul Tillich
Lord, when we come into your presence,
help us to be conscious of our sinfulness
so that we recognise how we are in fact grasping,
unjust, adulterous, like all human beings,
no different from the sinners we see before us;
and help us to know that our fasting and the tithes we pay
are not worth mentioning.
Then lead us to the deeper level
where we are content to stand at a distance from you,
not daring to raise our eyes to you,
but beating our breast and saying,

'God, be merciful to me a sinner.'
When we have made that inner journey
we go home knowing that we are at rights with you.

*'The only real prayer is the one in which we are no longer aware that
we are praying.'* St Anthony
Lord, once we start making a fuss about our prayers,
we find we start talking about good deeds
and pointing fingers at people.
Teach us to keep our prayer simple,
> - standing at a distance so that we do not draw attention to
> ourselves;
> - not daring to raise our eyes lest we disturb you;
> - beating our breasts because we do not feel to look down on
> anyone.

*'Those who know their own weakness are greater than those who have
seen the angels.'* Isaac of Nineveh, Syrian monk of the 7th century
Lord, many people feel burdened by guilt,
imagining that you are angry because they have no good deeds
for which they can stand in the temple and thank you.
Send them Jesus to remind them
that if they stay right where they are
and ask for your mercy they will go home at rights with you.

Lord, there are many things which divide people today:
race, culture, education, work.
How sad it is that our worship of you should also divide us.
Going to the temple should be a moment when we do not dare
to raise our eyes to look down on anyone,
but just beat our breasts and say,
'God, be merciful to us sinners.'

*'Our knowledge of God is paradoxically not a knowledge of him as the
object of our scrutiny, but of ourselves as utterly dependent on his saving and merciful knowledge of us.'* Thomas Merton
Lord, we thank you for moments
when we feel no desire to raise our eyes,
because we do not want to understand or even to question you,
only to experience that you are merciful to us sinners.

Lord, self-righteousness is very insidious.
Even when we try hard to avoid it,
we find that we are self-righteous about our spiritual progress.
We thank you for spiritual guides who, like Jesus,
can perceive the subtle ways
in which we pride ourselves on being virtuous
and despise everyone else.

Lord, forgive us that as a church we are like the Pharisee,
proud that we are virtuous and despising all other churches,
reminding ourselves of their faults, which we avoid,
and of the good things we achieve.
Be merciful to us sinners.

Lord, we pray for church leaders and political leaders.
They make great efforts to impress us
by telling us of the faults they avoid
and the great things they do,
whereas they are never more at rights with us
than when they ask us to forgive them their sins.

'What worries me ... is the growing invisibility of the poor.' Timothy
Radcliffe, Master General of the Dominican Order
Lord, our modern world glorifies those who have made it in life
– their faces are always on television,
their names in the headlines,
and as a church we often follow this trend.
Help us to focus rather on exalting the humble.

'I rejoice, my brothers and sisters, that our church is persecuted
for its efforts of incarnation in the interests of the poor.' Archbishop
Romero
Lord, we pray that your church may seek only the exaltedness
which Jesus promised to those
who make themselves one with the lowly.

All Saints

Gospel reading: Matthew 5:1-12

¹*Seeing the crowds, Jesus went up the hill. There he sat down and was joined by his disciples.* ²*Then he began to speak. This is what he taught them:*

³*'Happy are the poor in spirit; theirs is the kingdom of heaven.*

⁴*Happy the gentle; they shall have the earth for their heritage.*

⁵*Happy those who mourn; they shall be comforted.*

⁶*Happy those who hunger and thirst for what is right; they shall be satisfied.*

⁷*Happy the merciful; they shall have mercy shown to them.*

⁸*Happy the pure in heart: they shall see God.*

⁹*Happy the peacemakers: they shall be called sons of God.*

¹⁰*Happy those who are persecuted in the cause of right: theirs is the kingdom of heaven.*

¹¹*Happy are you when people abuse you and persecute you and speak all kinds of calumny against you on my account.*

12 *Rejoice and be glad, for your reward will be great in heaven; this is how they persecuted the prophets before you.'*

On this feast day we are invited in Year C to reflect on St Matthew's version of the Sermon on the Mount, Jesus' long discourse which runs from chapter 5 to chapter 7. If the Sermon on the Mount summarises the teachings of Jesus' public ministry, the Sermon itself is summed up in the Beatitudes.

Doing lectio divina on the Beatitudes is a different exercise from reading a book on them. There have been many excellent books on the Beatitudes in recent years.* No matter how helpful such books are, reading them is not the same as doing lectio on the Beatitudes. With a book our aim is to grasp the message of the Beatitudes; with lectio divina the aim is similar but the method different. We focus on the text, get to love it (perhaps for the first time) and let it lead us to love the Beatitudes. As a result

---

*One of the best (in my opinion) being *'The Beatitudes - Soundings in Christian Tradition'* by Simon Tugwell OP (Darton, Longman & Todd, 1980).

the text engages us. Our response to it is not merely 'What a beautiful message!' but 'What a beautiful text!' and 'It has touched me deeply!'

The *Jerusalem Bible* version introduces each beatitude with the word 'happy'. This is an unfortunate translation which the *New Jerusalem Bible* has corrected by returning to the traditional 'blessed'. Even with 'blessed' we need to give it its full biblical meaning. It includes being 'happy' (an aspect which was neglected in the past) but adds the notions of 'specially chosen by God' and 'a blessing for others'.

The Beatitudes are 'wisdom teaching', a biblical literary form that our church has tended to neglect in recent centuries. Jesus is reporting facts, not moralising. At no point does he say, 'You should do this.' He says, simply, 'People like this are blessed' and lets us draw our own conclusions. We respond by entering into the truth of the passage – not 'Jesus is telling me to do this', but 'This teaching is true.'

The wisdom is celebratory and our meditation must be the same. Each beatitude begins with an exclamation – 'How blessed!' I must modify the previous point therefore. Our response is not 'This teaching is true' but 'How true it is!' and even, 'How wonderful that it is true!'

Wisdom is universal by definition. The Beatitudes are teachings in human living, valid not for Christians only (still less for Catholics only) but for 'all men and women of good will', an expression used by all recent popes in their social teaching. We must make sure that our meditation leads to universal conclusions – 'All gentle people have the earth for their heritage', 'All who are pure of heart see God', and so forth.

As always with lectio divina, the text is intended to be in dialogue with our experience. The Beatitudes throw light on our experience and our experience explains the Beatitudes. Our response is not merely 'This is true' but 'This helps me to understand this parent, friend or teacher who touched my life very deeply' and in turn, 'This person helps me understand the Beatitudes.'

Referring to concrete experience is specially important with the Beatitudes which are expressed in biblical language that is foreign to us, e.g. 'poor in spirit', 'hunger and thirst for what is right', 'pure of heart', etc. Especially with such expressions, we need to start with our experiences of people and let them explain the meaning of the beatitude, e.g. 'My mother was the kind of person to whom the kingdom of heaven belongs, so being poor in spirit means being like her.'

Jesus himself is the prime example of the Beatitudes in practice. We should apply them to him, basing ourselves on some incident reported in the gospels.

The Beatitudes constitute a whole. They are seven (in the Bible, the number indicates perfection) aspects of the model human being – for us Christians, the Jesus way of being human.

There is a movement between the seven so that the full picture of the ideal human being unfolds gradually, one beatitude leading spontaneously to another, until we grasp the entire teaching in its complex harmony.

It would be a mistake, however, to look for these connections too quickly; our reflection would end up 'heady' rather than 'celebratory'. We take one beatitude at a time (any one), stay with it for as long as we are comfortable and then allow the connections with others to emerge in our consciousness, so that they are all contained in the one.

This will take time and we shouldn't hurry the process. At any one stage in our lives we will find that one beatitude is particularly dear to us. We must be in no hurry to move to another. Perhaps one lifetime is not long enough to love them all – and in any case when we go to the Father we will see them as one.

In the Bible (as in all great religious traditions) we enter wisdom through paradox. Things that are usually opposed are reconciled at a higher level, giving us new insight – and new joy.

The Beatitudes are paradoxes and we must make an effort to read them as such which is difficult because they have become familiar and no longer surprise us. If a beatitude does not surprise (even shock) us, it means that we have lost its meaning.

The paradox is in two 'movements' (like the movements of a symphony):

a) A main section brings together two 'opposites':
- 'poverty of spirit' and 'possessing the kingdom';
- 'gentleness' and 'having the earth for one's heritage';
- 'mourning' and 'being comforted', etc.

The bringing together is simultaneous. We weaken the Beatitudes when we make the second a 'reward' for the first. The bringing together must be based on experience. The question in each case is, 'When have I seen these two things combined in one person?'

b) Having seen the combination, we exclaim 'How blessed!' (in the wide sense explained above).

The Beatitudes are generally interpreted as a teaching on the interior life, and so they are. This must be correctly understood however. According to biblical spirituality, our inner dispositions are reflected outwardly, not merely in one-to-one relationships but in every area of human living, including public life, international relations, etc.

Some commentators make a distinction between inward and outward looking beatitudes:

a) three are 'inward looking': poor in spirit, mourn, pure in heart;

b) four are 'outward looking': gentle, hunger and thirst for righteousness, merciful, peacemakers, being persecuted.

We must not make too much of this distinction however. All the beatitudes speak of inner dispositions which are reflected outwardly. What we must do is give the beatitudes their full scope, seeing them as ideals of human behaviour at every level:

- our relationship with God;
- one-to-one relationships as parents, friends, teachers, spiritual guides;
- leadership style in church or secular communities;
- relationships between communities within nations and nations within the human family.

Below are a few brief comments to help you start your meditation.

Verses 1 and 2 give the setting of the Sermon. They remind us that every gospel passage, even a long discourse like this one, is a story. It is never a text book reading, a disembodied 'voice' speaking to us from an indeterminate place. We read it as a story then, asking ourselves (from our experience as always) who has been the Jesus who 'began to speak' to us in this vein.

Verses 3 to 12 can be divided

a) 3-10: a main section which proclaims the 'blessedness' of the Jesus way;

b) 11-12: a small section outlining its negative aspects.

Verse 3:

This first beatitude summarises them all. We will experience this by seeing how it is lived in each of the others. The two sides of the paradox are:

a) 'poor in spirit' which means not being attached to anything less than the absolute;

b) 'theirs is the kingdom of heaven' means attaining the absolute; this can have as broad a meaning as we wish to give it, e.g. union with God, a wonderful human relationship, a harmonious community.

Verse 4:

a) We must make sure to relate 'gentle' to concrete experience; e.g. it must include being 'non-violent' in one form or another.

b) The 'earth' can be taken literally, giving the beatitude an ecological meaning but we can also interpret it as a community.

Verse 5:

With this beatitude especially we must not set a time lag between the two aspects of the paradox. Jesus' teaching is that only those who know how to mourn will experience true comfort.

Verse 6:

'What is right' is an unfortunate translation. The traditional 'righteousness' is better. It means God's plan of harmony for ourselves as individuals and for all communities, including the entire human family.

Verse 7:

We can interpret 'have mercy shown them' of the response of others, 'people will show them mercy'. Or we can take it as a Jewish way of saying, 'God will show them mercy'. In either interpretation it is a 'paradoxical' statement. We often think that the way to have people on our side is by inspiring them with fear, and believers tend to think that God is pleased with them when they take a hard line.

Verse 8:

We give a wide interpretation to both sides of the paradox. 'Pure of heart' means being free from every form of ego-centredness. 'See God' means being conscious of the divinity in every person and situation.

Verse 9 is paradoxical for the same reason as verse 7.

In verse 10 again 'right' is better translated as 'righteousness'.

Verses 11 and 12:

Here again we must give a correct interpretation to the future tense. The contrast is not between present and future but between the inner peace of believers and the turmoil which surrounds them.

* * *

'When I was, he was not, now he is, I am not.' Hindu sage
Lord, how true it is that
when we are poor in spirit, your kingdom is ours.

'I can be saved only by being one with the universe.' Teilhard de Chardin
Lord, forgive us that we look on the earth
as an enemy to be conquered.
Teach us to be gentle so that we will experience the earth
as a precious heritage that we come home to.

'If you love God the pain does not go away but you live more fully.'
Michael Hollings
Lord, forgive us that we are afraid to mourn
and so don't experience your comfort.

*'The ideals which have lighted my way and time after time given me
new courage to face life cheerfully have been kindness, beauty and
truth. The trite subjects of life – possessions, outward success, luxury –
have always seemed contemptible.'* Einstein
Lord, forgive us that we no longer
hunger and thirst for your righteousness
and so are never satisfied.

'We don't possess the truth, we need the truth of the other.' Bishop Pierre
Claverie, French Dominican Bishop killed by fundamentalist Muslims in Algeria
Lord, lead us to the blessedness
of looking at others with compassion
and then experiencing their compassion for us.

*'Whether it is the surface of Scripture or the natural form of nature,
both serve to clothe Christ, two veils that mask the radiance of his faith,
while at the same time reflecting his beauty.'* John Scotus Eriugena
Lord, free your church
from all that takes away our purity of heart
and clouds our vision:
- focusing on showing that we are superior to others;
- trying to be popular with our contemporaries;
- being concerned with increasing our numbers.
Lead us to purity of heart so that we may see you at work
in every person and every situation.

*'Once you have rid yourself of the fear of the oppressor, his prisons, his
police, his army, there is nothing they can do to you. You are free.'*
Nelson Mandela
Lord we thank you for peace makers;
they are truly your sons and daughters.

*'Truth must be protected at all costs but by dying for it, not by killing
others.'* Lactantius, 4th century
Lord, forgive us that we are afraid
of being abused and persecuted
and having calumny spoken against us.
Help us rather to rejoice and be glad
when these things happen to us,
and to know that we will have a great reward,
and that this is how they persecuted the prophets before us.

Thirty-First Sunday in Ordinary time

Gospel reading: Luke 19:1-10

¹Jesus entered Jericho and was going through the town ²when a man whose name was Zacchaeus made his appearance; he was one of the senior tax collectors and a wealthy man. ³He was anxious to see what kind of man Jesus was, but he was too short and could not see him for the crowd; ⁴so he ran ahead and climbed a sycamore tree to catch a glimpse of Jesus who was to pass that way. ⁵When Jesus reached the spot he looked up and spoke to him: 'Zacchaeus, come down. Hurry, because I must stay at your house today.' ⁶And he hurried down and welcomed him joyfully. ⁷They all complained when they saw what was happening. 'He has gone to stay at a sinner's house' they said. ⁸But Zacchaeus stood his ground and said to the Lord, 'Look, sir, I am going to give half my property to the poor, and if I have cheated anybody I will pay him back four times the amount.' ⁹And Jesus said to him, 'Today salvation has come to this house, because this man too is a son of Abraham; ¹⁰for the Son of Man has come to seek out and save what was lost.'

This Sunday's passage tells the story of Jesus' meeting with Zacchaeus. It is a very touching story, full of character, so deep that we are always finding new things in it, treasures we had not noticed before. God, however, did not write the story for us to admire St Luke's extraordinary artistry as a storyteller, but so that we could recognise ourselves in it and discover how he has been and continues to be at work in the world.

There are three characters in the story: Zacchaeus, Jesus, and the complainers. Each of these is a universal symbol; all people and all communities have lived the three stories at one time or another. In your meditation then, you are free to identify with any of them – though not at the same time.

Zacchaeus is the symbol of those who experience that 'salvation has come to their house.' The word 'house' invites us to recognise that it 'comes' to both individuals and communities.

'Salvation' is a word we Christians use frequently but it has become very vague. This is not a happy state of affairs; it means that we have no practical way of evaluating whether we are 'saved' or not, and so we can easily deceive ourselves. The Pharisee in last Sunday's gospel thought he was saved, but was not, and we must be 'on our guard' against falling into the same error. The story of Zacchaeus tells us – as always, speaking to our experience – 'this is what happens when salvation comes to a house.'

We know from our faith that final and complete 'salvation' will 'come to our house' only at the end of time. In the course of our lives what we have are temporary and partial experiences of salvation. These are very significant, however, since they
   - give us a glimpse of what the final experience will be like (Jesus' teaching based on experience, as always);
   - are a pledge that we will experience it.
The story of Zacchaeus tells us that 'salvation' is an experience of healing and reconciliation, so deep that we exclaim with gratitude in the words of Jesus, 'Today salvation has indeed come to this house,' or 'Yes, God really seeks out and saves what was lost.'

As individuals, we remember times when quite unexpectedly we felt accepted and loved
   - by the other members of our family,
   - by God in prayer, at a retreat or a Life-in-the-Spirit seminar,
   - by friends,
   - by fellow workers in our work place,
   - by the other members of our profession.
We felt able – perhaps for the first time – to 'stand our ground' and speak up for ourselves, affirming who we were, our past failures and the good deeds we intended to do.

We celebrate 'salvation moments' for communities too:
   - a local church is converted to the cause of the poor and wel-comes them into its inner life, renouncing power and pres-tige, ignoring the comments of sceptics;
   - an ethnic group which had been discriminated against is now fully accepted as part of the community;
   - religious groups, enemies up to now, are reconciled and commit themselves to work together;
   - on the occasion of a tragedy (e.g. September 11) a nation is warmed by the sympathy of the human family;
   - labour and management experience reconciliation in the work place.

The details of the story invite us to retrace the steps which lead to the moment of 'salvation'.

a) The tentative start: Zacchaeus was 'too short' – he was not up to meeting Jesus as an equal. The 'sycamore tree' he climbed was a safe place from which he could peep out; the most he could hope for was to 'catch a glimpse' of Jesus.

b) The moment of grace: he experienced Jesus 'looking up' at him, and heard those wonderful words, 'Come down, hurry, because I must stay at your house today.' This represents the time when we no longer feel isolated; we can invite Jesus (in whatever form we meet him) into our home, not at some time in the vague future but 'today'. We feel totally free, do what we have to do without anyone having to tell us. Like Zacchaeus, we are no longer 'too short' but can 'stand our ground'.

c) 'They all complained when they saw what was happening': how real this is! Salvation is never a simple process, it always has a negative side – a 'letting go' of something that was holding us back. We continue to hear voices from the past (parents, teachers, priests, nuns) telling us that we are 'sinners', not good enough to have Jesus stay at our house. Now we hear another voice telling us that they are merely 'complaints,' not the truth. God's truth about us is that we too are 'children of Abraham.' We celebrate the Jesus person who said that to us.

Jesus is the symbol of the care-giver, the one who 'comes to save what was lost,' 'bringing salvation to houses' by inviting the marginalised (communities and individuals) into the mainstream.

Here again we must not allow ourselves to be vague.

We know of many instances where preachers ended up dehumanising individuals and communities instead of 'bringing salvation to their houses.' In this story Jesus teaches us by example, 'This is how a Son of Man brings salvation.'

We think of

- parents or grandparents with children who are shy or withdrawn;
- teachers with slow students;
- parish leaders, clerical or lay, with 'backsliders';
- managers with employees who are awkward and are forever doing or saying the wrong thing.

We think too of those who do something similar for groups, reaching out to those who are alienated;
- Israelis to Palestinians and Palestinians to Israelis;
- between Catholics and Protestants in Northern Ireland;
- in work places where industrial relations have broken down.

Jesus proceeded in steps, each of which we can identify with and celebrate.

a) He 'looked up'. This is very significant; he was 'going through the town' but still found time and energy to notice Zacchaeus hiding in the tree.

b) 'Come down', meaning 'let's talk as equals.' 'Hurry, I must stay at your house today.' The invitation is spontaneous and unconditional; it invites mutuality. There isn't the slightest trace of condescension. Jesus is saying, 'I need your help now.'

c) 'Today salvation has come to this house.' Here again no condescension, it is a moment of celebration.

d) 'This man too is a son of Abraham.' Jesus makes an 'option for the poor', he consciously and deliberately protects the poor against the 'complainers'.

e) The 'Son of Man came to save what was lost.' In the light of the above, we can see that he is neither possessive nor condescending; he 'saves' by providing the right environment so that Zacchaeus decides of his own accord to be the best he can be.

The complainers are ourselves when we are mean and self-righteous. We are like them as individuals; as the church; as members of a social class, race, ethnic group, or nation.

This is a story of grace. We are not meant to condemn them but to identify with the journey Jesus is inviting them – and us – to make:

a) The starting point is the 'complaint': 'He has gone to stay at a sinner's house.' The basic problem is personal insecurity, as we know from experience. We can identify two ingredients:
- we cannot bring ourselves to celebrate the blessings enjoyed by those who differ from us, belonging to a different religion, social class, ethnic group or ideological position;
- our thinking is static, we do not allow for growth on the part of those we have categorised as 'sinners' – failures in some way.

b) The end of the journey is when we are able to say, 'He too is a Son of Abraham.' We celebrate the person (or it could have been an event) who led us along that journey.

How we respond to the story of the complainers will depend on our present situation. We can

- celebrate that we have made the journey as individuals or as a community (thanksgiving),
- become aware that Jesus is calling us to make the journey (repentance),
- recognise that the journey will be very demanding (petition).

* * *

'God communicates himself to all persons, redeems them and stamps their being with an orientation towards sharing his life.' Karl Rahner
Lord, we thank you for the people who have been Jesus for us.
When we felt inadequate, too short,
so that we could only catch a glimpse
of that dream we had for ourselves,
you sent someone who looked up
and saw more in us than we ourselves did.
They were not aggressive, didn't force themselves on us,
just said they were happy to stay in our house.
We felt a surge of joy within us.
We knew that others were calling us sinners,
but that didn't stop us,
we felt free to stand our ground,
confess whatever wrong we had done
and commit ourselves to making a new start.
Salvation came to our house that day,
we knew that we too belonged to the family of Abraham
and experienced that you came to seek out
and save what was lost.

'The most terrible walls are the walls that grow in the mind.' Nelson Mandela
Lord, we pray that your church in every country
will be more like Jesus in seeking out those who are lost.
Teach us when we go through our towns to look up and notice
those who like Zacchaeus have made an appearance

but hide themselves because they feel inferior
and want merely to catch a glimpse of us.
Teach us to stay with them in their houses
and so bring out the best in them
so that they may experience
that they too are descendants of Abraham.

*'The Word of God is red-hot iron. And you who teach it, you'd go pick-
ing it up with a pair of tongs lest you burn yourself.'* Georges Bernanos,
Diary of a Country Priest
Lord, forgive us for when we do not believe
in the power of the gospel to save what was lost.
We have written off people as sinners,
but if we had taken the trouble to stay in their houses
we would have seen salvation come there.

*'The captains, merchant bankers, eminent men of letters,
Distinguished civil servants, chairmen of many committees,
Industrial lords and petty contractors all go into the dark.'*
T. S. Eliot, *The Four Quartets*
Lord, we thank you for the artists and poets who remind us
that we are all sinners
and we can have no grounds for complaint
when we see your saints staying at a sinner's house.

*'Emancipate yourselves from mental slavery.
None but yourselves can free your minds.'*
Lord, forgive us for preaching salvation
in a way that is possessive.
We pray that like Jesus with Zacchaeus
we may assure those to whom we want to bring salvation
that we need their hospitality
so that they may stand their ground
and choose freely the way of salvation.

Thirty-Second Sunday in Ordinary Time

Gospel reading: Luke 20:27-38

[27] *Some Sadducees – those who say that there is no resurrection – approached Jesus and they put this question to him,* [28] *'Master, we have it from Moses in writing, that if a man's married brother dies childless, the man must marry the widow to raise up children for his brother.* [29] *Well then, there were seven brothers. The first, having married a wife, died childless.* [30] *The second* [31] *and then the third married the widow. And the same with all seven, they died leaving no children.* [32] *Finally the woman herself died.* [33] *Now, at the resurrection, to which of them will she be wife since she has been married to all seven?'* [34] *Jesus replied, 'The children of this world take wives and husbands,* [35] *but those who are judged worthy of a place in the other world and in the resurrection from the dead do not marry* [36] *because they can no longer die, for they are the same as the angels, and being children of the resurrection they are sons of God.* [37] *And Moses himself implies that the dead rise again, in the passage about the bush where he calls the Lord the God of Abraham, the God of Isaac and the God of Jacob.* [38] *Now he is God, not of the dead, but of the living; for to him all men are in fact alive.'*

The gospel passage for this Sunday is challenging for us who practice the lectio divina method of reading the Bible text in dialogue with personal experience. From the outset there are three problems we must deal with if the passage is to speak to our experience as it is intended to.

a) The general theme of the passage is resurrection from the dead, something we believe in faith but have not experienced. We must therefore take the same approach as we did with 'salvation' in last week's passage; we start with partial and temporary 'resurrections' we have experienced and allow them to become glimpses of the final and complete resurrection at the end of time. 'Dying' will then refer to times when our world – or that of others – collapsed, and 'resurrection' to times when we (or they) experienced new life in the wake of failure.

b) The passage refers to the Leviticus law in Deuteronomy 25:5, which is based on an understanding of marriage that is very different from ours. We Christians don't see marriage in those terms at all. Our meditation will have to be very creative therefore, and we will probably find it impossible to use the word 'marry' in praying the passage.

c) Some of the sayings in the passage are vague: 'children of this world,' 'children of the resurrection,' 'they are like the angels,' 'sons of God,' 'to him all are alive.' In each case we must let the Word come alive by interpreting it in the light of our experience.

Through meditation, then, we will be led
- to celebrate 'children of the resurrection,' including ourselves when we are at our best (thanksgiving);
- repent of our lack of faith in the resurrection, as individuals and as a church (humility);
- pray that faith in the resurrection will triumph in us, in the church and in the world (petition).
The passage is in three sections.

1. Verse 27: Introduction
The introduction sets the scene – a meeting between Jesus and the Sadducees; we can identify with both.

a) Jesus is in a specific historical situation. He is in Jerusalem, knowing that he is about to be arrested and condemned by the leaders of his own people and abandoned by his closest associates, but still self-possessed and trusting. In this encounter with the Sadducees he is not merely teaching, but bearing witness to his own faith in the resurrection. He 'leads us in our faith and brings it to perfection' (Heb 12:2). In our meditation we celebrate him and those who have been his presence for us, challenging us by word and example to renew our faith in the resurrection.

b) The Sadducees are ourselves to the extent that we 'say that there is no resurrection,' not in words (since the resurrection is part of our Christian faith), but in practice. What this implies is explained below.

2. Verses 28 to 33: a case study
The Levitical law is far removed from our experience, so we have to be creative in interpreting it. Like all biblical laws, this was a life-giving Word of God. In the culture of the time, however,

it reinforced the lowly status of women. Women at that time found their identity in having children. A woman who had no husband – and therefore no children – was nobody. Her inferior status is summed up in the Sadducees' question 'To which of them will she be wife?' which can be interpreted as 'She has no husband, so who will she be?'

This approach is typical of people who 'say there is no resurrection'. We fall into that category when we define people by their achievements – jobs, bank accounts, popularity, prestige, fame. We look scornfully at those who have none of these things – or lose them by 'dying'. Like the Sadducees asking 'To which of them will she be wife?' we ask the poor and vulnerable, those who are old or sickly or who have experienced failure, 'Who are your friends? What have you produced?' Many still look on women as the Sadducees did; they ask, 'Whose wife is she?'

In setting priorities for ourselves we 'say there is no resurrection' when we get involved in projects not because they are good in themselves but because they bring us 'outer' benefits such as making money and attaining high positions, or 'inner' benefits like feeling good about ourselves, feeling superior to others or having a sense of achievement.

The problem in each case is that we allow ourselves to be defined by these accomplishments. If we were to lose them ('die'), we would have to ask, 'Who am I?'

We do this also as communities: the church and its organisations and religious orders 'say there is no resurrection' when they become fixated on achievements – attracting large numbers, attaining moral perfection, and so forth. Suppose we became 'a little flock' again, we would be asking ourselves, 'Are we really the church?'

The capitalist system with its emphasis on productivity and consumption 'says that there is no resurrection'. Nations too can seek their identity in military or economic victories, saying 'What makes us a great nation is that we are No 1.'

3. Verses 34 to 38: three wisdom sayings

Jesus answers the Sadducees' – and our – question with three wisdom sayings intended to evoke the response, 'How true!' and 'How wonderful!'

a) Verses 34 to 36

Jesus distinguishes between 'children of this world' and 'children of the resurrection' (there is a bit of both in each of us). 'Children of this world' focus on achievements. 'Taking wives and husbands' does not refer primarily to marriage (and not at all to Christian marriage). It means getting involved in projects in such a way that they define us. We do that when

- we sacrifice important values to attain high positions for ourselves and our families;
- we scheme and connive to prove ourselves better than others;
- we make 'being perfect' the goal of our spiritual life so that when we fall into sin we become 'nobodies'.

To the question 'Whose wife will she be?' Jesus replies, 'She was never just "somebody's wife"; she was a person in her own right! So what if all her husbands died. She is still who she is.' This is the attitude of 'children of the resurrection,' those who are 'judged worthy of a place in the other world'.

Here again 'they do not marry' does not refer to marriage as we understand it. It means, like Jesus himself, not allowing one's identity to be determined by achievements. We can imagine Jesus saying to the Sadducees: 'I too committed myself to many people (the leaders of the people, the Pharisees, Judas) and I have little to show for it. You think I am a failure, but I don't see myself that way at all.' He told the apostles the same thing on the night before he died: 'You will all run away, leaving me alone; but I am not alone because the Father is with me' (Jn 16:32).

We think of the great men and women of our time who give themselves to noble causes such as non-violence, harmony between religions, liberation of oppressed people, equality for women. Often they are not praised, are condemned even, but continue to live fulfilled and productive lives. They are 'children of the resurrection,' they 'cannot die,' they are 'sons and daughters of God'.

We think too of 'children of the resurrection' who give themselves to the service of others:

- parents who walk with children who are mentally challenged;

- friends who continue to care for delinquents;
- political leaders who renounce power rather than compromise principles.

They often do not see tangible results, their sacrifices seem useless and 'die'. But they maintain their dignity, their sense of self worth, their sense of humour even – they 'cannot die'. If we ask them, 'Who are you?' they will answer like Jesus, 'I am a son or daughter of God.' Like Jesus they teach us to understand what it means to be 'the same as the angels.'

b) Verses 37 and 38a

Jesus further clarifies his teaching on resurrection by inviting the Sadducees (and us) to enter into Moses' experience in 'the passage about the bush'. This refers to moments when we sense the greatness of people who have touched our lives ('ancestors' in the widest sense). They died, failed, or did not receive due recognition but continued to 'live'. They could do this because they were 'alive to God'. We may be dead in the eyes of our fellow human beings, but if we are true to the best of ourselves, we are alive in the eyes of God. The passage reminds us that faith in God is what gives us human beings the power to transcend failure and humiliation.

c) Verse 38b widens the scope of the teaching. Not merely our 'ancestors' (in the wide sense as above) but all men and women have within them the seed of immortality, the potential to be truly great, 'alive to God'.

We celebrate moments when some 'Jesus' helped us – by word and example – to understand these things.

* * *

'This great disaster is a symbol to us to remember all the big things of life and forget the small things of which we have thought too much.'
Jawaharlal Nehru, speaking to the Indian people on the night Gandhi was assassinated

Lord, we worry so much about what will happen
to what we have worked for:
- will our children put into practice what we have taught them?
- will the community project we started survive?
- will we remain in good health?
- will our political party win at the polls?

We are like the Sadducees who say there is no resurrection.
But now and then you send us Jesus
to remind us that the only really important thing in life
is to be judged worthy in your sight,
and then we are truly children of the resurrection
and we cannot die.

*'Raise me up Lord, until at long last it becomes possible for me in per-
fect chastity to embrace the universe.'* Teilhard de Chardin
Lord, free us from petty concerns,
that the whole world may be alive to us as it is to you.

*'The fulfilment of our destiny is to find in God all our individual and
personal reality.'* Thomas Merton
Lord, forgive us for accepting the notion
that we fail as human beings when we are not productive:
>   - we make parents feel inferior because they have no child-
>   ren, or because their children are not successful at school or
>   in the work place;
>   - we are envious of fellow professionals who have attained
>   greater heights than us;
>   - we do not give full respect to the aged in our communities;
>   - we lose enthusiasm for what we are doing because our
>   worth is not recognised by others.

We are Sadducees who say there is no resurrection.
Give us the grace to approach Jesus and receive his word
challenging us to move from being children of this world
to becoming children of the resurrection,
your sons and daughters.

'Is it worth it? Everything in life is worth it if the heart is not small.'
Leonardo Boff
Lord, we thank you for faithful people,
>   - those who remain faithful when their spouses are not;
>   - parishioners who are content to work for the community
>   without acknowledgement;
>   - those who fight for a noble cause without success.

They often die childless,
but we know you judge them worthy of a place with you
in the resurrection from the dead.

Lord, we thank you that, like Moses,
we can call you the God of our ancestors,
from Africa, India, Europe or the Caribbean.
Many of them didn't have our faith,
things we hold dear were not important to them,
but they are alive to us, because they believed in you
and you are not the God of the dead but of the living.

'Human beings ought not to consider their chances of living or dying.
They ought only to consider on any given occasion whether they are
doing right or wrong.' Socrates
We thank you, Lord, for sending us in every age
men and women like Jesus,
who challenge us to be children of the resurrection,
to know that we cannot die
once we are concerned to be alive to you.

'To the conquistadors, where there were no wonders there was nothing.'
V. S. Naipaul
Lord, we your church ask your forgiveness
for the times we judged cultures
by their wealth and military might,
forgetting that to you they were alive – your sons and daughters.

'The church admits that she has greatly profited and still profits
from the antagonisms of those who oppose her.'
Vatican II document on The Church in the Modern World
Lord, we thank you for people who come to us
as the Sadducees came to Jesus.
At first their objections seem foolish,
but then we find that they help us clarify what we believe in.

Thirty-Third Sunday in Ordinary Time

Gospel reading: Luke 21:5-19

5*When some were talking about the Temple, remarking how it was adorned with fine stonework and votive offerings, Jesus said,* 6*'All these things you are staring at now – the time will come when not a single stone will be left on another: everything will be destroyed.'* 7*And they put to him this question: 'Master,' they said, 'when will this happen, then, and what sign will there be that this is about to take place?'* 8*'Take care not to be deceived,' he said, 'because many will come using my name and saying, "I am he" and "The time is near at hand." Refuse to join them.* 9*And when you hear of wars and revolutions, do not be frightened, for this is something that must happen, but the end is not so soon.'* 10*Then he said to them, 'Nation will fight against nation, and kingdom against kingdom.* 11*There will be great earthquakes and plagues and famines here and there; there will be fearful sights and great signs from heaven.* 12*But before all this happens, men will seize you and persecute you; they will hand you over to the synagogues and to imprisonment, and bring you before kings and governors because of my name* 13*– and that will be your opportunity to bear witness.* 14*Keep this carefully in mind: you are not to prepare your defence,* 15*because I myself shall give you an eloquence and a wisdom that none of your opponents will be able to resist or contradict.* 16*You will be betrayed even by parents and brothers, relations and friends; and some of you will be put to death.* 17*You will be hated by all men on account of my name,* 18*but not a hair of your head will be lost.* 19*Your endurance will win you your lives.'*

This gospel passage is a collection of many different sayings of Jesus, all of them relevant to a situation of crisis in the present or looming in the future. You will recognise their truth from your experience of small as well as big crises.

In verses 5 and 6 the people are typical of us when we allow ourselves to be seduced by earthly glory, and Jesus is the voice of God reminding us of how short-lived it is.

You can take verse 7 with the preceding passage – we admit that earthly glory is short-lived but at least we want to know when it will end – or with verse 8, which describes the yearning for easy solutions to a deep crisis.

Verses 10 and 11 are typical of Bible teachings on the necessity of suffering before salvation.

Verses 12 to 15 show us the followers of Jesus trusting like him in the midst of persecution.

Verses 16 to 18 are promises that their trust is well founded, as his was.

Verse 19 is a little gem of a saying, true of life at every level.

* * *

Lord, we quite rightly wonder at human achievements today:
- the exploration of outer space and of subatomic particles;
- supermarkets and shopping centres stocked with goods of every kind;
- all the modern means of communication: faxes, satellite television, the internet.
They are the temples of our modern world
and we are like the disciples of Jesus,
remarking how they are adorned
with fine stonework and votive offerings.
Remind us that all these things we stare at,
the time will come
when not a single stone will be left on another.

'We remain in the midst of contradiction, in peace, knowing that it is fully solved, but that the solution is secret and will never be guessed until it is revealed.' Julian of Norwich
Lord, we remember times of deep crisis in our lives:
- a family break-up;
- we fell back into a sin we thought we were done with;
- we could not get out of depression;
- a national crisis seemed without solution.
Many came with easy solutions, saying, 'This is it!'
and promising that the time of deliverance was near at hand.
But you sent us someone like Jesus
who told us not to be frightened,
that these things must happen and the end was not so soon.

'The church is still there. Everyone else may have moved, but the church is right in the centre.' Josephite priest in Los Angeles, May 1992
Lord, we thank you that in many parts of the world
where there are wars and revolutions,
where nation is fighting against nation
and kingdom against kingdom,
where there are earthquakes and plagues
and famines here and there,
fearful sights and great signs from heaven,
the followers of Jesus are not frightened
but remain where they are and continue to do his work,
knowing that these things are things that must happen,
but the end is not so soon.

'Politics encircles us like the coils of a snake from which one cannot get out no matter how much one tries. I wish therefore to wrestle with that snake.' Gandhi
Lord, we thank you for those who enter public life
unafraid that they will be brought to judgement by everybody,
seeing it rather as an opportunity to bear witness.

'We may not be able to dictate to the world, but we must speak to the world out of our own frame of interpretation.' Lloyd Best, *Carifesta V*, August 1992
Lord, we who belong to smaller nations
often feel ourselves standing before
the great powers of the world and being judged by them.
Give us the grace to discover the wisdom and eloquence
that you yourself have given us
and that no one can resist or contradict.

Lord, when we are young we think
that we become great through our achievements.
Life has taught us the truth of Jesus' words:
it is by endurance that we win our lives.

The Feast of Christ the King

Gospel reading: Luke 23:35-43

35*At that time the leaders jeered at Jesus, saying: 'He saved others, let him save himself if he is the Christ of God, the Chosen One.'* 36*The soldiers mocked him too, and when they approached to offer him vinegar* 37*they said, 'If you are the king of the Jews, save yourself.'* 38*Above him there was an inscription: 'This is the King of the Jews.'* 39*One of the criminals hanging there abused him. 'Are you not the Christ?' he said, 'Save yourself and us as well.'* 40*But the other spoke up and rebuked him. 'Have you no fear of God at all?' he said. 'You got the same sentence as he did,* 41*but in our case we deserved it: we are paying for what we did. But this man has done nothing wrong.* 42*Jesus,' he said 'remember me when you come into your kingdom.'* 43*'Indeed, I promise you,' he replied, 'today you will be with me in paradise.'*

In order to enter into the celebration of today's feast, two points need to be clarified. The first concerns the meaning of 'kingship' in this context. In modern Western culture, kings and queens do not exercise much power; in the Bible, however, their power is absolute. What we are celebrating in today's feast, then, is the power of Jesus – who never used his power to his own advantage.

Secondly, this power, real and effective though it is, is very different from power as the world understands it. We must not therefore presume that we know what we are celebrating. The feast is rather an occasion to discover (or re-discover) the power of Jesus, how it works and what are its effects, so that we can celebrate it.

The rediscovery will be a true celebration as we experience that Jesus' way of exercising power – the divine way – is good news for us as individuals and as communities, including the entire human family. It will also be a call to conversion as we become aware of how little this kind of power is known and practiced, even by Jesus' followers. We will also feel a longing for the coming of God's kingdom – a new civilisation based on this kind of power.

We repent for the way we Christians have misrepresented

the power of God, portraying him to the world as a despot, and often a cruel one, 'not fully mirroring the image of our crucified Lord, the supreme witness of patient love and of humble meekness' (*Tertio Millennio Adveniente*).

It is an occasion to celebrate the great models of Jesus-power of our century. We remember concrete scenes: Gandhi clothed in his homespun dhoti, standing before the British viceroy; Pope John Paul on his first visit to Poland as pope; Nelson Mandela leaving prison; Mother Teresa standing alongside Princess Diana. The power of truth, of honesty, of forgiveness – with no frills! How different the world would be if it was governed by this kind of power.

We are led to consciousness of Jesus' power through lectio divina. Meditating on the Bible text we remember with deep gratitude moments when people entered our lives exercising his kind of power; other moments when by God's grace we have been able to exercise it ourselves, as parents, church ministers, fellow-workers, friends. These moments are for us 'seeds of the kingdom.'

This year, the gospel reading on this feast day invites us to enter into the extraordinary paradox – Jesus exercises power as he hangs on the cross. We enter the lowliness first – at the level of our feelings, as always in lectio divina. We feel for Jesus hanging between two criminals, 'one on the right and the other on the left,' as St Luke puts it dramatically in the previous verse; there is no question of Jesus' cross being slightly higher than the others, as in some representations of the scene. He is mocked by the leaders and the soldiers and by one of the criminals. Their humiliating taunt is true: he saved others, now he cannot save himself. We allow the text to remind us of similarly humiliating situations.

Our meditation then moves in one of two directions. We can celebrate great people who, like Jesus, enter freely into that lowly state so that they can exercise his power:
- leaders share their weaknesses with members of their communities;
- religious men and women choose to live among the poor and the vulnerable;
- groups like Alcoholics Anonymous have as their basic principle that all members must confess their addiction;

- the church confesses its sins to other religious bodies and to the world.

More often people are brought into that situation – usually against their will – and by their faith they make it an experience of Jesus power:

- parents remain faithful to their children even when they see the children sent to prison, victims of drugs, rejecting their parents' values;
- spouses maintain their dignity when deserted by their partners;
- we grow in compassion through falling into a sin we thought we had done with;
- our church becomes more humble as it becomes engulfed in sex scandals;
- a political party is able to purify its goals because its members have been discovered to be corrupt.

The passage invites us to celebrate the effect of Jesus power: the lowly are lifted up, 'set in the company of princes' (Ps 113:8).

The good thief is the perfect symbol of this process, and we must enter with deep emotion into his moment of grace. Up to then he was nobody. Now, because Jesus shares his lowly fate, he has his moment in history, he enters into his truth. Jesus thanks him for his faith (how he needed that!) and they enter into paradise together, companions in faith.

We can read the passage from either perspective – that of Jesus or that of the thief. We celebrate times when our failures brought us into communion with those we looked down on; other times when someone we were in awe of shared their story with us and we discovered our own greatness, perhaps for the first time.

It would be good to spend some time letting ourselves be touched by the setting of the story. This is a unique moment in human history – God's power at its height; a sacred moment, too, when the great high priest is reconciling the world to God. But what do we see? Two human beings standing by each other, nothing more! What a judgement on how the world judges greatness – or holiness – whether of people or of places!

* * *

Lord, we thank you that you showed us in Jesus
the true meaning of power.
He exercised kingship by coming among us as a companion,
sharing our terrible experiences of lowliness,
of hanging on a cross with two criminals,
one on our right and the other on our left,
having people jeer at us that we who are your anointed,
specially chosen by you,
we who in many ways bring salvation to others,
are unable to save ourselves or our families.
Now we can share with you the pain
of having those who looked up to us
as leaders in the community
angry with us because we could not save ourselves
and them as well.
Give us the grace to follow in Jesus' footsteps,
turning our moments of lowliness into moments of power,
when we enter into communion with those in need,
proving the values of the world wrong,
for when we learn to accept that we cannot save ourselves,
we bring salvation to all those who are being crucified.

Lord, we pray that your church
may not stand aloof from the world,
but be willing like Jesus to share the fate of the poor,
to accept hanging on the cross with them,
alongside criminals at times, some on the right, some on the left.
Hanging there, your church will experience
mockery as Jesus did,
from religious leaders as well as ordinary foot soldiers,
will be abused by those
who look for quick solutions to their problems,
but will discover heroic people
among those whom the world has condemned
and will enter paradise walking hand in hand with them.

Lord, we thank you for people
who have been for us what the good thief was for Jesus.
Whereas others rejected us because we could not save them,

They saw that we had done nothing wrong
to deserve the harsh sentence we had received,
called us tenderly by our names
and asked us to be remembered among our friends.

Lord, we thank you for addicts who join rehabilitation groups
like Alcoholic Anonymous.
Like the good thief,
they experienced disgrace but continued to fear you.
Then one day they stopped abusing others for their plight
and recognised that they deserved
the sentence of condemnation they had received
from family and friends,
and that they were paying for the evil they had done.
Very humbly,
they turned to the Jesus you sent to share their pain
and asked to be admitted into the company of the converted.
They received the assurance that on that very day
they would enter into your kingdom.

Lord, we pray for those who feel excluded
      - from positions of power because they have failed
       in their professional or personal lives,
      - from the church because of failures in their personal rela-
      tionships.
We pray that they will discover greatness
and holiness in themselves
by contemplating Jesus on Calvary
      - a king with no royal throne,
      - a priest with no temple or altar of sacrifice,
just himself and the good thief in their integrity,
willing each other into paradise.

18 A Palmiste Dr 2218429
6576195
Lazzari Lands
Phillipine

888 3861
to try to die
DIE